FAITH
with
FOCUS

How to Live Your Life with Passion and Rule It with Reason

BRIAN MANGINES, J.D., LL.M

Published by:
FWF Publishing, LLC
BOCA RATON, FLORIDA

Copyright © 2019 Brian Mangines

ISBN-13: 978-0-578-46187-8

Editing: Carol A. Rosenberg
www.carolarosenberg.com

Cover and interior design: Gary A. Rosenberg
www.thebookcouple.com

Printed in the United States of America

"For the ones who had a notion
A notion deep inside
That it ain't no sin to be glad you're alive."
–BRUCE SPRINGSTEEN

and

To my mom and dad, who lived with passion
but ruled their lives with reason

and

To my wife, Mimi,
who has always been there for me,
and to our three children,
Austin, Lindsay, and Megan

CONTENTS

WHO ARE YOU?

*"Well, who are you?
I really wanna know."*

"WHO ARE YOU," THE WHO

FOR MANY YEARS, IN THE BACK OF MY MIND, I knew that someday I would write a book. And yet, as is the case for virtually everyone else and everything else in life, the timing never seemed right. There always seemed to be another matter that was more pressing, like a work deadline. Business pressures, financial strain, my children's sporting and school events, and other life situations kept me away from writing. Then there were the all-important sporting events I needed to watch on TV, which also dragged me away from my goal of writing a book. Even though I had a few stops and starts along the way where I actually committed words to paper, I made very little progress. One day, though, I *decided* that if I was ever going to manifest my vision of becoming an author, I needed to *start now to invest the time* to chip away at writing my book.

While I had many concepts that I wished to convey in my book, based upon personal experience and observation, I lacked a clear-cut direction. Eventually, I took a three-ring binder and compiled all my tidbits and began to organize them into subject matters. Initially, I had several titles for my book in mind: *The Invisible Hand; Money, Magic, Music, and The Law of Attraction;* and *Life's a Game, Play It Well* to name a few. Over time, an order and identity to my words began to emerge. Thus, I chose to title my book, *Faith with Focus: How to Live Your Life with Passion and Rule It with Reason.*

My philosophy of faith with focus has been reinforced and vetted by the hundreds of self-help books I have read, the audio recordings I have listened to, and the seminars I have attended. "Faith With Focus" has become my own personal battle cry and one that I often impart to my clients. I am an attorney by trade and over the course of my more than twenty-five years as a lawyer, I have counseled many individuals who were facing a major crisis in their lives, including terminal illness, death of loved ones, injury, employment law/discrimination matters, divorce, litigation, business loss, foreclosure, and bankruptcy. My practice has evolved into estate planning and probate. The former practice areas were reactive in nature while estate-planning practice is proactive. I prefer the latter.

I routinely tell my clients to maintain faith through their darkest moments and to let me focus on their legal situation. In other words, if they focus, or I should say, refocus, on the things that made them successful in the past, the rest will take care of itself. Their legal issues I can resolve. When I began to represent many hundreds of clients in bankruptcy/foreclosure defense, I quickly realized I was in the "faith with focus" business as much as the legal business. My ability to inspire and encourage my clients boosted their faith and focused their attention on what really mattered. I gave my clients hope while encouraging them to focus.

Most of the inspirational self-help books I have read break into one of two categories. They are either the "woo-woo, have faith, life is magical, and everything will be perfect" books, which are laden with faith and inspiration but typically provide very little step-by-step direction. The other type of self-help book is more of a technical manual of how to live your life in a practical way (e.g., save and invest your money for a rainy day). In my mind, to be truly fulfilled, one must strike a balance between simple blind faith without adequate planning and living a life of reason. Finding that balance has been a struggle for me personally, although now that I consciously follow my inner light, which I discuss in chapter 1, the path has become clearer. In other words, there is not only universal truth but a universal order that I contend is divine, and that divine order permeates throughout our universe.

In this book, I wish to invite you to discover or strengthen your own faith (however you define that word), assist you in focusing on areas of your life that need improvement, suggest practical ways to correct your shortcomings, put you on a path heading in the right direction, and ultimately allow you to find inner peace and harmony through love of God, self, neighbor, and life itself: a tall order, I know.

It is said that books aren't written; they are rewritten. At one point, I misplaced my three-ring binder. However, I made a *definite decision* to keep writing rather than use the lost binder as a convenient excuse to halt my dream. Like other first-time authors, I have at times struggled with self-doubt. *Who am I to write this book? What do I have to offer that has not already been covered by other more talented authors and speakers? What will make my message unique? Who will read this book and who will really benefit from it?*

Well, the fact is that I do have a unique perspective on life, having experienced it from my different angles: youngest of eight children, lawyer, business owner of a multimillion dollar enterprise, and then failed business owner—and then successful comeback business owner. I have assisted hundreds of people through the darkest days of their lives as a result of job loss, business failure, divorce, death of loved ones, foreclosure, and bankruptcy, and I have witnessed many people rebound to regain economic stability and peace of mind. Along the way, I have observed personality traits that have emerged that helped individuals regain their faith in themselves. As a trust and estate attorney, I have come full circle, and I have gained perspective on how those who live with abundance think and act, maintain or increase wealth, and protect their legacy.

"We learned more from a three-minute record, baby, than we ever learned in school."
"NO SURRENDER," BRUCE SPRINGSTEEN

I love music. Who doesn't? The vibration of music touches our souls. Music moves us physically, emotionally, intellectually, and spiritually. Music makes us feel, and music makes us think. From my youngest days, I have always relished listening to song lyrics and finding meaning in and application of them to my own life. In high school and college, I would often daydream and write my own lyrics during class. I have continued to write songs off and on over the years. I play no musical instrument, and I have been booed off karaoke stages, but through the power of faith with focus, I have a published song called "Main Street Symphony." It is a collaboration with an award-winning songwriter, Molly-Ann Leikin. (The power of love in action.)

Since the physical, spiritual, and intellectual power of music is universal, I have decided to begin and end each chapter of this book by quoting song lyrics to emphasize my thoughts. Additionally, I also reference the Bible and scientific literature, and draw upon the words of great thinkers and philosophers. This brings me to one of the main themes of the book. Music is a combination of thought and passion. And it is that elixir of passion and thought that produces a powerful force. When we properly integrate passion with solid reasoning into our lives, we not only find purpose and meaning but also find truth through accomplishment. Universal truth reveals itself in many forms—there is a universal truth, and if we follow its light, we will achieve what we conceive. Universal truth is not random; rather, it comes from divine order. When we purposely direct our focus toward universal truth, we find our true purpose. When we maintain faith in that purpose and keep our focus on it, we find true enlightenment.

Life is not as complicated or as intricate as our mind—if left untamed—makes it seem. For this reason, I have included very simple exercises at the end of each chapter. Very few of the exercises require actual writing, although you may wish to convert your thoughts into writing as there is power in the written word. Instead, the exercises require simple tasks that can be undertaken immediately and continuously, such as smiling. Some exercises require contemplation with the aim that you will arrive at your own conclusion about what "faith with focus" means to you.

If you are ready to find out who you are and what your purpose and passion in life are, then let's put the ball in play and as the band the Cars say, "Let the good times roll."

"This is our life, this is our song."
"WE'RE NOT GONNA TAKE IT," TWISTED SISTER

CHAPTER ONE

THE LIGHT

"This little light of mine, I'm gonna let it shine,
Let it shine, let it shine, let it shine."

"THIS LITTLE LIGHT OF MINE," JOHN LOMAX

"THERE'S A LIGHT THAT SHINES WITHIN ME, and I know that it shines in you too." I first wrote those words back in 1989, in my mid-twenties, as the opening line of a love song that I wrote to my then-girlfriend, Mimi. The words came to me while listening to music in a dimly lit tavern in Hartford, Connecticut. It was the night before Mimi was to return from her seven-week study abroad in Europe. As I sat on a barstool, I felt the undeniable presence of a light glowing inside me. That night and those words did *not create* my inner light, for it had always been there. Instead, that one simple sentence *revealed* my light to me. I had discovered my light man-ifested through love.

Mimi and I have been married now for almost 30 years. We have three beautiful children, Austin, Lind-say, and Megan. How could I have ever known back then that the opening lyric to my love song would serve as the first line of chapter 1 of my first book? Mimi and I have been through a lot together during our years, but through all the ups and downs, the thrills and spills, and the twists and turns, I have never lost consciousness of my inner light. Indeed, my inner light has taken on new meaning. That is how life works.

The truth is that we all have a light that shines within us. Whether you are a songwriter with beautiful melodies and lyrics, an artist with magnificent colors waiting to burst forth, or an author who waxes poetic, there is a light that resides within you. You may be a laborer, a homemaker, an executive, or a preacher. You may hail from America, China, Europe, or India, but you have a light. You may be rich or poor, healthy or sick. You may be tall or short, overweight or thin, good looking or homely,[1] but you have a light. The light, whether you are aware of it consciously or subconsciously, is unmistakable. Your light is part of a universal radiant energy field. Your right as a human and, indeed, your life purpose is to access your light and let it shine through in everything you do. That is all you must do.

WHAT DOES "THE LIGHT" MEAN TO YOU?

What words do you think about when you hear the term "the light"? Is it love? Peace? Joy? Warmth? Harmony? Brightness? Serenity? Happiness? Goodness? God? Is it all of these things? What feelings are triggered when you hear of the term "the light"? Are they the same words you think about when you hear the term? In both my private conversations and while speaking publicly about the light, I have come to recognize that some people understand immediately what I am referring to and others are clueless about "the light." The phrase "the light" carries different connotations for different people. Many who understand the light simply can sense it more than they can define it. I am one of those people.

For me, the light comes in two parts. First, it is a natural radiant energy field that beams within me love, harmony, happiness, awareness, and connection to the Universe. Second, it is my natural inclination toward the person I was meant to be as expressed through my natural talents. My light provides faith, is faith, and provides focus, is focus. It is easier for me to feel my light than to describe it. It is a spiritual and effervescent presence that allows me to see things in a more spiritual realm. My light serves as my inner GPS, providing me direction and clarity, hence focus. Take a few moments now and contemplate what your light feels like, what it means to you, and whether you can see it and feel it.

> *"The 'light' is consciousness. Consciousness is one, manifesting in legions of forms or levels of consciousness. There is no one that is not all that is, for consciousness, though expressed in an infinite series of levels, is not divisional."*
>
> NEVILLE GODDARD

When you become aware of your light, you have taken the first step on the path toward enlightenment.

When you allow your inner light to guide you, you no longer need to live on what Wallace Wattles, in his book *The Science of Getting Rich,* labeled "the competitive plane," but rather you can exist on "the creative plane." The competitive plane causes conflict and anxiety and eventually leads to defeat. The creative plane frees your mind to engage in activities that benefit you and others around you. It allows you to grow as a human mentally, spiritually, and physically. Do not compare yourself to others. When you follow your light, you feel good and you feel fulfilled. You manifest your destiny.

From this moment forward, always be conscious of your light in everything you do. Let your light be your beacon as a lighthouse is to a ship. The darker and the stormier the weather, the more valuable and essential your light becomes. When life is tough and appears to be dark, know that it is the outside circumstances around you and not your life that is dark. Focus your attention on your light. Keep your light on and let it shine regardless of your present circumstances, and it will reveal your life's purpose to you, it will protect you, and it will guide you. Life really is that simple.

> *"But everything exposed by the light*
> *becomes visible*
> *—and everything that is illuminated*
> *becomes a light."*
> EPHESIANS 5:13, NIV

Your inner light is divine, and you are divine light. The light comes from our "Maker," whom I personally call God. You may wish to refer to the "Maker" as the "Universe," "Infinite Intelligence," or some other term used to describe an organizing force of consciousness that permeates the galaxies. This force brings light and order to our existence. Everything in existence is comprised of the same substance of energy that some modern-day physicists refer to as the "God Particle."[2] The uncovering of the God Particle—essentially an invisible energy field that permeates the Universe, which in turn is present in all physical matter—confirms the teaching of the Bible wherein it is said: "For since the creation of the world God's invisible qualities—his eternal power and divine nature—have been clearly seen, being understood from what has been made, so that people are without excuse." (Romans 1:20, NIV). The light emanates from our Maker and therefore God is within you. You are part of God. Your light is universal, and it lies within and without all of us. God has given you light because he made you light; use it.

If you are already aware of your inner light, then know that your light can be intensified as easily as a gas burner on a stove top can be turned up. If you do not feel the light and have never felt it—feel it now. All you need to do is call for it and it is there. The easiest way to call for your light is to lift your chin and smile. Roald Dahl said, "If you have good thoughts, they will shine out of your face like sunbeams and you will always look lovely." For a life on purpose means following and using your light. When channeled in the right direction, you live a purposeful and meaningful life free from bundled confusion in your mind. You bring sunshine to others as well.

Dante said that "a mighty flame followeth a tiny spark." My purpose in writing this book is not simply to let my own light shine, but to provide a spark so that you can let your light radiate throughout the world. Better yet, join your light with the light of others and you indeed have a mighty flame. When enough collective light is joined together and focused in the direction of a compelling purpose, the light becomes indomitable. Nothing can or will stop it. How else do you think the American Revolution was launched and won?

Whether your sphere of influence is small or large, you are a magnificent being and your light can bring warmth to everyone and everything within your sphere. You have a force field, and that force field draws in people, circumstances, and events into your life like a magnet attracts steel. What's more is that your light shall always destroy the dark for it is written that "the light shines in the darkness, and the darkness has not overcome it" (John 1:1-18, NIV).

It is not the *quantity* of your light (i.e., how big it is), but rather the *quality* of your light that matters the most. Your light may warm only one soul on just one occasion, yet that single touch of light may be so profound to cause a shift in that person who then discovers his or her own light. It may be your spouse, your child, a friend, or a stranger. Your light, so long as you allow it to do so, will bring forth the light in others. Bring your light into focus and you have purpose.

Your light is yearning to shine through to the outside world. Perhaps you are conscious of your light and you already allow it to shine through all you do. If that's the case, then allow your light to intensify. On the other hand, you may feel as though your light is barely lit. If that's the case, then take a moment to feel your light shine. What is one way that you can let it shine to the outside world? Can you smile as you pass by a stranger? Can you compliment someone today? Know that any small act of kindness creates positive energy, and you can continue to build upon that energy as your day unfolds. If you are reading these words and wondering whether it is worth it to keep allowing your light to shine, I can assure you it is. I have been there, but I am back. That dark place of hopelessness is part of my journey, and now looking back, it was not as dire as things seemed at the time. It never is. Know always that you are enough just the way you are now.

There are, however, two types of light. There is friendly fire, and there is destructive fire. Fire can warm and protect us from the cold, and it can be used to cook our meals. It can also destroy the forests, a mighty building, or even an entire town. Since your light comes from God—is God—it is your responsibility to use your light in a way that serves others and our Universe. This is what the Bible calls "free choice."

Our light may be revealed in many ways. I have a friend Larry. Larry is the kind of person many people don't quite know what to make of when they first meet him. He has a tendency to do or say things that defy social norms. His comments, though, are good-natured and well intentioned. Once you get to know Larry, you realize he has a heart of gold. The more you get to know Larry, the more you feel his light. He reminds me of the Pink Floyd song "Shine On You Crazy Diamond." Some would say Larry is a diamond in the rough, but rough or not, Larry is a diamond and he shines. The fact that he is in the jewelry business and sells diamonds is not coincidental in my mind. He has a beautiful wife and two beautiful daughters. One was a star soccer player at a major Division I school, and the other has a budding advertising career. How does Larry's light shine in the world? Here is a text message that Larry received from his youngest daughter: "Dad, I think the reason that I'm so cool is because you're so cool." That is pretty cool to me.

Larry is radiant because he is unafraid to naturally let his light shine. Are you a diamond in the rough? Many of us are. We don't allow ourselves to shine because we haven't been taught to shine. We are afraid to shine because we are worried of the negative feedback we will receive from others. Rather than act with forceful energy, we instead tiptoe through life to make sure we don't step on others' toes. Alternatively, we let others control our direction and they keep us on our heels. Be not afraid! Start right now to walk through life on the balls of your feet.

Virtually all proper athletic positioning requires the athlete to play while being on the balls of their feet. This is where your energy and power come from. When you are talking to someone, remain on the balls of your feet. While working, remain on the balls of your feet. By simply standing on the balls of your feet, standing (or sitting) up straight, keeping your chin up and smiling, you can gain positive energy, focus, and confidence. Your light will flow outwardly. You can shine like Larry, too, if you *decide* and *allow* yourself to use your light. Get in tune with your light.

Burning desire comes from the light. The same burning desire that drove all the great achievers of this world, Shakespeare, Da Vinci, Mozart, Lincoln, Gandhi, Martin Luther King Jr., and our spiritual leaders came from the same light you have. For burning desire to manifest, it must be fueled by faith. Where there is faith there is light. When the light is directed—or focused—in a specific direction, it intensifies like a magnifying glass can intensify a ray of sun. Passionate love is the strongest form of light. The moment passionate desire is mutual between human beings, it ignites the light and fire erupts. When you fall in love, life suddenly becomes magical and you flow easily and happily with the Universe. Is it any wonder then why so many great love songs have been written?

What is faith? It is not a simple recantation of a religious creed that has been drilled into us, though that type of faith can reinforce your inner faith. It is not a mere wish for something to happen, for wishes do not burn the way faith does. Faith is that inner impetus that comes from the certainty that you are teamed up with a greater force and together you can break down any obstacle or barrier and get from where you are to where you want to be. Your light is your beacon of faith. Follow the light with razor-like focus and you will have faith. If you have faith, you will have courage. If you demonstrate courage in your daily living, you can—and will—light the world on fire.

The problem, of course, is that most of us have been conditioned not to let our inner light shine through the way we want it to. From an early age, most of us have been conditioned that someone else or something else controls our destiny. All that changes when you decide that from this moment forward you will rekindle your light, you will intensify its flame, and you will bring it forth. In this way, your light can project as an outward sphere of light and all those around you will be drawn to it. As long as you allow your light to shine, you are successful in your own right. Therefore, you need not try to outshine others. When others try to outshine you, or worse, dampen your flame of enthusiasm, simply feel your light shine. Remember, the light destroys the dark.

A flame flickers, meaning that it is always in motion. Your light is dynamic, too. It grows and dwindles along with your emotions and your whims. If you are determined to do so, you can deliberately choose to intensify your light and let it grow. Growth is more than just a state of being—growth is an emotion, and when joined with your light, it increases exponentially. Growth is a choice. You must get intentional. Use your light. Have faith in your light. Focus your light. Growth leads to a breakthrough. Growth comes from faith with focus.

Shakespeare wrote, "To thine own self be true." What is the light? The light is love. The light is the truth. The light is your truth. Stick to the things you love, stay committed to your inner truth, and "the truth shall set you free."

EXERCISE

➢ Spend time connecting with your inner light, or if you already have discovered your light, seek to intensify it. (You may wish to go to a quiet place, close your eyes, and then imagine a ball of light illuminating within you and then filling up the entire room.)

➢ Begin thinking about how you can use your light to help yourself and others. How can you use your light? Does it make you feel stronger and instill faith in yourself? Does it shine light on a problem you may be facing?

➢ Today, for the rest of the day, and as often as you can, keep your chin up and smile. When you see someone, smile. When you think of someone— friend or foe—smile. When you approach a task, smile. Feel the smile emanate from your inner light.

➢ Stand and walk on the balls of your feet.

➢ Get in tune with your light and let your light shine no matter what the day may bring.

➢ Let your light radiate love, peace, harmony, joy, prosperity, and health to all you meet.

➢ Spend a few minutes focusing on what the word "faith" means to you. Then as you go through your day, remain vigilant to your faith.

➢ Spend a few minutes today focusing on your light. What makes you glow on the inside?

➤ What makes you shine on the outside?

➤ What things about you receive the most compliments from others?

➤ **Extra Credit:** Listen to the song "Let It Shine," and feel your light shine as you listen.

"I see your true colors
And that's why I love you
So don't be afraid to let them show"

"TRUE COLORS," CYNDI LAUPER

CHAPTER TWO

THE VISION

*"Now here I go again, I see the crystal visions
I keep my visions to myself."*

"DREAMS," FLEETWOOD MAC

I DON'T EXACTLY KNOW WHAT STEVIE NICKS of Fleetwood Mac was referring to when she used the phrase "crystal visions," but I do know that we all have visions in our head. For Stevie, they appear to be "crystal," which is a powerful vision to behold. Do you have crystal visions or are they faded visions of what could have been? What are the visions you are keeping to yourself? Do you keep visions to yourself that you could crystalize and then allow them to shine through to the outside world? And, if you did allow these visions to shine, could they be life changing both for you personally and for others who might benefit from your crystal visions?

Whether we are conscious or unconscious of it, each of us holds pictures in our minds. The power of these visions cannot be understated. They are driving our lives, our thoughts, our actions, and our emotions.

The vision we hold in our mind determines our future. Most of us, as Bruce Springsteen says, play the "same old played out scenes" in our heads each day. Worse, most of the time we are oblivious of the reasons why we think what we think. That is because most of us simply do not *deliberately* select and direct the movie that plays out in our head. Others deliberately select them for us though. Teachers, parents, coaches, bullies, friends, lovers—all have a script lined up for us.

By casting your light on your vision, by recognizing that you have the power to choose the images you hold in your head, you will change your life. This is the essence of both faith and focus. Creating a vision for your life the way you want it to be means consciously deciding what you want to accomplish and what you want to be in your life. This is a nondelegable duty. When you tap into your light, you can readily create a vision that harmonizes with your life's purpose:

"If we are to survive, we must have ideas, vision, and courage. These things are rarely produced by committees. Everything that matters in our intellectual and moral life begins with an individual confronting his own mind and conscience in a room by himself."
ARTHUR M. SCHLESINGER JR.

Emerson said that we are what we think about all day long. Painting a strong vision in your mind (drawn by your light) is the first stepping-stone toward living the life that is meant for you and made by you. No one ever achieved anything great in the outer world until they saw it for themselves privately inside their heads. Architects who design blueprints saw the building in their heads before they translated it onto paper. The songwriter, the author, and the poet all visualized themselves writing before they ever set pen to paper.

"Because faith in facts can help create those facts."

ALICE FULTON, CORNELL UNIVERSITY
PROFESSOR OF ENGLISH AND POETRY

Sports are a great analogy for life. Throughout the course of a season or a game, there are inevitable ups and downs, twists and turns, wins and losses. But through it all, the spirit (the light) emerges and champions are made. Since sports serve as a metaphor for life, I will draw upon a few sports examples to illustrate my point about the power and importance of having a vision.

Jim Valvano was a big dreamer. Born in New York to two Italian immigrants, Coach Valvano had an enormous presence about him. I never met Jim Valvano, but I sense he instinctively must have known that he had light. He cast his bright light with great intensity and he cast it far and wide. Jim Valvano was not afraid to use his light. He also had visions and big dreams inside of him long before he ever coached the 1983 North Carolina State's men's basketball team to the national championship. In fact, the 1983 North Carolina State's men's basketball team lives on as one of the greatest stories in the history of American sports—indeed, it has transcended sports.

When Jim Valvano first became the head coach of North Carolina State in 1980, he had a single dream—to win the national championship. The first time he met his new players at NC State, he shared his dream of winning a national championship with them. He gave them focus. How far did he take it? Well, each year Jim had one practice that involved no basketballs. There were no defensive or offensive drills, and he did not teach any basketball fundamentals. Instead, this one practice session was devoted to only one thing during the entire practice. It was the tradition of climbing a stepladder and cutting down the nets from the basketball rim with a pair of scissors after winning a championship. Coach Valvano furnished the team with a pair of scissors and all the team did during this one practice was practice cutting down the nets.

The team *pretended* they had just won the national championship, and then they cut down the nets to celebrate their national championship. They not only physically cut the nets down, but they did so with full emotion just as if it were real. They jumped up and down. They cheered, hooted, and hollered. Notice that Jim took his dream to the outside world. He devoted an entire practice to cutting down the nets. At first, the players did not fully act as if it were real. But as the Wolfpack's then-center Thurl Bailey explained, "After a while when you practice something over and over it begins to feel real."

Keep in mind that this was an era when college basketball was at its peak. In its own conference alone, the Atlantic Coast Conference (ACC), NC State was competing against the likes of University of North Carolina with Michael Jordan, Sam Worthy, and legendary coach Dean Smith. Virginia was led by seven-foot-four-inch Ralph Sampson. Outside of the ACC were teams like Georgetown with Patrick Ewing as its star. It was an era when it was not uncommon for a player to stay and play all four of his college years before turning pro. It was a highly competitive era for college basketball.

At first, Jim Valvano's brash style was not well accepted by the more stoic college coaches. But he never hesitated to shine his light on his vision of winning a national championship for his players to see. Over time, his players began to share the same vision that Jim had. The vision did not immediately manifest despite the intensity of the vision. There was adversity. The team did not even reach the NCAA tournament after Valvano's first year, but still he kept his vision strong. In his second season at NC State, the team made it to the NCAA tournament but lost and was eliminated in the first round. Valvano and the Wolfpack kept dreaming and kept their ritual of devoting a practice each year to cutting down the nets.

By the time the 1983 season rolled around, Jim Valvano's dream seemed nothing more than a dream that was not going to come true. Things got worse when, after a strong start to the season, the Wolfpack's senior point guard, star, and team leader, Dereck Whittenburg went down with a broken foot. It was not certain if he would ever play college basketball again.

Then two weeks before the end of the season, due to his own faith and focus, Whittenburg returned.

Surprisingly, the Wolfpack won the ACC Tournament and advanced to the NCAA tournament. They won their first game and their second and then their third game to amazingly reach the final championship game. They had one big problem. They had to face the mighty Houston Cougars who were nicknamed "Phi Slamma Jamma" for their high-flying superstars like Clyde "The Glide" Drexler and Hakeem "The Dream" Olajuwon. Many were calling the Houston team the best college basketball team of all time.

The game was close. It was 52-52 when the Wolfpack's Lorenzo Charles rebounded Dereck Whittenburg's air ball shot (which he contends was a pass) and dunked it at the buzzer to win the 1983 championship. It is perhaps the most memorable moment in all of NCAA basketball tournament history. Jim Valvano was frantically running around the court with his arms raised high in search of someone to hug! The NC State team, led by their magnanimous coach, cut down the nets! They won the national championship. What had begun as a vision and a ritual of cutting down the nets became the real thing. Indeed, faith in facts can help create those facts!

Tragically, Jim Valvano would later die of cancer at the age of forty-three. He never lost his light though. Instead, he redirected his light on a new vision. At the first ESPY Awards ceremony, Jim accepted the inaugural Arthur Ashe Courage and Humanitarian Award. During his acceptance speech, he announced the creation of the V Foundation for Cancer Research, an organization dedicated to finding a cure for cancer. He announced that the foundation's motto would be

"Don't Give Up . . . Don't Ever Give Up." He concluded with a memorable quote: "Cancer can take away all of my physical abilities. It cannot touch my mind, it cannot touch my heart, and it cannot touch my soul. And those three things are going to carry on forever." Well Coach V, they have.

Today, even in physical death, Jim Valvano's light and vision shine brighter than ever. Through its research efforts, the V Foundation makes it possible for others struck with cancer to envision and manifest their dreams. What began as a vision of cutting down nets ultimately led to the creation of the V Foundation, which has helped millions of cancer-stricken individuals bring their visions to the outside world. Thank you, Coach V—your light and your vision will shine forever.

Fast-forward to 2014 when a young Kevin Ollie, in only his second year as a head coach (with no prior coaching experience at any level), led his seventh seeded Connecticut Huskies to the Final Four and ultimately the NCAA National Championship. How did Kevin Ollie bring such a low seeded team there? To be sure, he did it with tremendous focus and preparation. It all started, however, with a vision.

When UConn played at Southern Methodist University (SMU) in Dallas early in the year, Coach Ollie brought his team to Texas Stadium, the site of the upcoming 2014 NCAA Final Four. He brought his team inside the arena and had them sit and visualize that they had advanced to the Final Four. Except for their first-round game against St. Joseph's, which they won in overtime, they were the underdog in every game in the NCAA tournament. Nonetheless, they beat Villanova (number two seed), Iowa State (number four seed), Michigan State (number four seed), Florida (number one seed), and then the immensely talented Kentucky Wildcats in the championship game. Kevin Ollie had a vision, shared it with his team, and then acted on it by bringing his players to the arena to visualize what they would later eventually do—win the championship and cut down the nets! Wow, talk about faith with focus!

Visualization is not limited to athletic prowess. Great actors know the power of visualization, and they understand the power that is generated from engaging in physical action that is consistent with their vision. In fact, there is a name for it: "character acting." These actors, such as Daniel Day-Lewis, stay in character while filming a movie—even while off set. For example, while filming the movie *Lincoln*, Daniel Day-Lewis, playing Lincoln, remained in character as Abraham Lincoln even when he was not on set. Maybe some people found it peculiar to see Mr. Lewis walk around town in Abe Lincoln garb, but then again, he has won three Oscars, including best actor, for his portrayal of Lincoln.

One of the most practical and effective uses of visualization can be found in Dr. Bob Rotella's book *How Champions Think in Sports and in Life*. He describes visualizing what your response will be in advance of a situation that you anticipate will become a challenging situation. When you embark upon a goal, chances are overwhelming that you will encounter obstacles along the way. For example, you may be trying to lose weight and your diet is working. You are more committed than ever and you feel great. Then one night you go to a party, and before you know it, you give into temptation and begin eating everything in sight. A couple of drinks and a couple of fat-laden appetizers have derailed your diet. The next day you slip away further from your goal and suddenly you are back to your old ways. It is no wonder why diets seldom lead to permanent weight loss. It is far more effective to visualize yourself at your ideal body shape and focus your energy on that vision until you begin to naturally behave in accordance with your vision.

Nonetheless, what if you had visualized in advance of the party what your reaction would be when you were offered the first drink? You can choose your response in advance: "No thanks, I'll have a Perrier instead tonight." Or maybe it's "OK, this will be my one drink tonight." Or maybe you want to let yourself go at the party so you scale back your calories in the days leading up to the party. The point is that you can anticipate the situation in advance and then visualize the response so when the moment of truth arrives you make the choice that works for you. This same concept works for sales professionals who can anticipate objections from prospects and circumnavigate them with predetermined scripts to overcome the stated objection.

If we can predetermine our outcomes by picturing it in our mind first, then why don't most of us do it? The reason is because sustained, habitual thought is one of the most difficult activities a human can be called upon to do. Decades ago, Nobel Peace Prize recipient Dr. Arthur Schweitzer was asked, "What is the biggest problem confronting mankind?" His answer was that "The trouble with men today is that they simply don't think."

I contend that one of the main reasons most of us don't think things through is because man, by nature, is lazy. For me, on the one hand, this largely diffuses the "Is man good or evil?" debate. To be sure, religions, societies, friends, and foes have debated whether man's nature is good or bad. The Bible teaches us that we are born with original sin: "If we say that we have no sin, we deceive ourselves, and the truth is not in us." (1 John 1:8-10, KJV). Modern Hinduism, as offered through Swami Vivekananda, on the other hand, adopts the philosophy that "the divine exists in all beings, that all human beings can achieve union with this 'innate divinity'; and that seeing this divine as the essence of others will further love and social harmony."[3]

Depending upon your point of view (i.e., focus), there is plenty of evidence to support either theory. The "man is good" group can readily point to the outpouring of generosity that follows a natural disaster. Humankind throughout the world unites in tragic situations. After the devastating Haiti earthquake in 2012, help from all over the world poured in. The United States alone offered aid in the amount of $466 million. Indeed, man is good, and this is why I personally believe that divinity runs through each of us (even if we are naturally lazy)!

On the other end of the spectrum, humankind has been plagued by violence. The mere mention of the names of the worst terrorists and brutal dictators (whom I refuse to grace by naming them) makes one shudder. Mass murders, riots, and senseless shootings on high school and college campuses, in nightclubs, and in airports have become part of our modern living. Wars in the name of religion or nationalism have lined the pages of history and continue to permeate our existence.

To me, man's most natural state is *laziness* until inspired or incentivized either by pain or pleasure. Since we tend to be lazy, we are easily influenced by outside sources whether those sources are positive or negative. Where we place our focus determines how we act.

> "Nothing can prevent your picture from coming into concrete form except the same power which gave it birth—yourself."
>
> GENEVIEVE BEHREND

It easier to read this book than do the things it suggests you do.

Our thoughts become our visions. Our mind is the most powerful force we have, yet it needs to be trained. It needs to be cultivated. Each thought is a seed. Good thoughts produce good fruit, but only if we tend to those seeds. Conversely, seeds of weeds grow weeds. The distinction is that weeds naturally grow rampant while most fruits need to be tended to. In fact, a garden left unattended will be overrun by weeds even if the productive seed has been planted.

Visionaries deliberately choose their thoughts and cultivate them. They keep their crystal visions to themselves for only so long, until soon they have others around them seeing the same thing they are seeing. They visualize things well before others do. Hence, they earn the label "visionary."

Driving experts teach that the most important thing to do when your car is spinning out of control is to keep your eyes focused on where you want to go. By focusing on a target in the distance in the direction you are headed, you will be able to instinctively redirect your car so that it is once again traveling in the right direction. Live your life the same way. Beginning with the end in mind, keep your vision focused on your intended result and you will start moving in the right direction even if it feels like your life is spinning out of control.

"You can't stop us on the road to freedom,
You can't stop us 'cause our eyes can see."
"TUPELO HONEY," VAN MORRISON

Starting now, you are going to choose freedom. You are going to use your light to brighten your vision. Choose your destination by going there in the mind first—the body will follow. In fact, it is always this way. General George S. Patton once said, "You have to make the mind run the body. Never let the body tell the mind what to do. The body will always give up." I first read this quote in a book about marathon running. I have used this quote to my advantage many times, not only when training for and running in marathons, but also throughout all aspects of my life. In the next chapter, we examine how your light and your vision can team up with another powerful force that lies within you—your voice. First, however, complete the following exercises.

EXERCISE

➤ Visualize a desired result with full emotion for at least five minutes every day using your light and imagine you already have whatever it is you want most in life.

➤ Visualize yourself as a champion cutting down the nets!

➤ Get in character when you visualize (act it out).

➤ Visualize an anticipated situation or obstacle you will encounter while reaching for one of your goals. Visualize your response to the situation obstacle in advance and, when the moment arrives, act per your predetermined vision. Dig deep.

➤ Have faith in your facts because your faith in facts will help you create those facts!

➤ Even if you feel like your life is spinning out of control, keep your eyes focused on where you want to go and you will automatically start heading in the right direction.

"Take your passion,
And make it happen,
Pictures come alive, you can
dance right through your life."
"FLASHDANCE," IRENE CARA

CHAPTER THREE

THE VOICE

"Listen to your heart
Never let the world's noise
Get louder than your own voice."
DAVID HALLYDAY

YOU HAVE A LIGHT AND A VISION that resonates within you. Your light and your vison give power to your inner voice, which is the omnipotent sounding board within you. You have control over the voice within you, but the voice is not you. You own your voice. Your voice does not own you, and no one else owns your voice unless you allow it, or them, to own it. Your voice derives its source from Infinite Intelligence. God gives us free choice. Your voice is not good or bad. Your voice either works for you and you direct it, or your voice works against you because you allow it to be your enemy. You get to choose how to use your voice. You also get to choose whether the voice you listen to throughout your life is your voice or the voice of others. My question to you then is "Whose voice do you listen to?"

Researchers tell us we have up to sixty thousand thoughts each day. These thoughts manifest in the form of the voice that runs through our heads. Moreover, the thoughts we hold are predominately the same thoughts each day. We run the same script in our head day after day and yet wonder why nothing changes. This is the one promise I will make to you: *Starting right now, change what your voice tells you each day, and you will change your life according to the story your voice tells you.*

There is an old Cherokee story about the battle that goes on within our own mind:

THE TALE OF TWO WOLVES

One evening, an elderly Cherokee brave told his grandson about a battle that goes on inside people.

He said "my son, the battle is between two 'wolves' inside us all. One is evil. It is anger, envy, jealousy, sorrow, regret, greed, arrogance, self-pity, guilt, resentment, inferiority, lies, false pride, superiority, and ego.

The other is good. It is joy, peace, love, hope, serenity, humility, kindness, benevolence, empathy, generosity, truth, compassion, and faith."

*The grandson thought about
it for a minute and then asked
his grandfather:*

"Which wolf wins?"

*The old Cherokee simply replied,
"The one that you feed."*

When you deliberately direct your voice *in a positive way,* you become a shining example of source. Begin at once to use your voice to empower you and not to disempower you. When you align your voice with your light and your vision, you can then begin to tell a new story of your life *the way it is meant to be.* This, in turn, begins to direct your subconscious mind. Focus your attention on words that bring with them light—like *faith, joy, strength, abundance, health, wealth, growth, prosperity, peace, love, harmony,* and *happiness.* Repeat these words often both out loud and internally throughout your day. Paint pictures of these words in your mind and *feel* the positive energy they bring. Intense and persistent focus on these types of words will, in time, destroy the dark negativity that words like *despair, hate, frustration, hopelessness,* and *fear* carry with them. Leave your fear behind. Instead, follow your faith.

Your voice derives its power from the *beliefs* you hold in your mind. These beliefs influence your inner voice and prompt you to act—or fail to act—in accordance with those beliefs. When you train your mind to believe in the things that are consistent with the story you create for yourself, when you place faith behind your beliefs, you then begin to take actions both consciously and subconsciously to bring your story to life. Focus on your story the way you want it to be.

Let's pause and look at the meaning of the word "belief," as expressed through different channels:

WHAT IS A BELIEF?

Merriam-Webster defines "belief" as "a feeling of being sure that someone or something exists or that something is true." (Notice that a belief is a *feeling* and not a *fact*.)

Dr. Alex Lickerman, M.D., provides keen insight into the beliefs that we hold in our heads:

The Two Kinds of Belief
Why Infants Reason Better Than Adults

Post published by Alex Lickerman, M.D.,
on April 24, 2011, in Happiness in this World

Simply, a belief defines an idea or principle which we judge to be true. When we stop to think about it, functionally this is no small thing: lives are routinely sacrificed and saved based simply on what people believe. Yet I routinely encounter people who believe things that remain not just unproven but which have been definitively shown to be false. In fact, I so commonly hear people profess complete certainty in the truth of ideas with insufficient evidence to support them that the alarm it used to trigger in me no longer goes off. I'll challenge a false belief when, in my judgment, it poses a risk to a patient's life or limb, but I let far more unjustified beliefs pass me by than I stop to confront. If I didn't, I wouldn't have time to talk about anything else.

What exactly is going on here? Why are we all (myself included) so apparently predisposed to believe false propositions?

The answer lies in neuropsychology's growing recognition of just how irrational our rational thinking can be, according to an article in *Mother Jones* by Chris Mooney. We now know that our intellectual value judgments—that is, the degree to which we believe or disbelieve an idea—are powerfully influenced by our brains' proclivity for attachment. Our brains are attachment machines, attaching not just to people and places but to ideas. And not just in a coldly rational manner. Our brains become intimately emotionally entangled with ideas we come to believe are true (however we came to that conclusion) and emotionally allergic to ideas we believe to be false. This emotional dimension to our rational judgment explains a gamut of measurable biases that show just how unlike computers our minds are:

CONFIRMATION BIAS, which causes us to pay more attention and assign greater credence to ideas that support our current beliefs. That is, we cherry pick the evidence that supports a contention we already believe and ignore evidence that argues against it.

DISCONFIRMATION BIAS, which causes us to expend disproportionate energy trying to disprove ideas that contradict our current beliefs.

Accuracy of belief isn't our only cognitive goal. Our other goal is to validate our preexisting beliefs,

beliefs that we've been building block by block into a cohesive whole our entire lives. In the fight to accomplish the latter, confirmation bias and disconfirmation bias represent two of the most powerful weapons at our disposal but simultaneously compromise our ability to judge ideas on their merits and the evidence for or against them.[4]

In their book, *Money and the Law of Attraction,* Jerry and Esther Hicks describe a belief like this:

> A belief is nothing more than a chronic pattern of thought, and you have the ability–if you try even a little bit–to begin a new pattern, to tell a new story, to achieve a different vibration, to change your point of *attraction.* The **Law of Attraction** is responding to your vibration, and you can easily change your vibrational point of *attraction* by visualizing the lifestyle you desire and holding your attention upon those images until you begin to feel relief, which will indicate that a true vibrational shift has occurred.

Singer/songwriter John Mayer wrote a song entitled "Belief" and describes a belief as:

> *"Belief is a beautiful armor,*
> *But makes for the heaviest sword."*

The sum and the substance of the foregoing is that beliefs can be manufactured out of whatever we wish to use to make them up. And once we accept an idea as being true, we cling to that belief and will gravitate toward ideas and evidence that support that idea. In fact, we will go out of our way to ignore evidence and will work to defeat ideas that tend to disprove our beliefs. Beliefs can protect us, they can build us, or they can hamper and even destroy us. The key, then, is to cherry-pick your beliefs and then start focusing on the evidence that supports those beliefs until your mind accepts those beliefs as reality and acts in accordance with them. Choose the beliefs that will raise you up and don't stop believing at the first sign of trouble!

> *"Don't give up on your faith*
> *Love comes to those who believe it*
> *And that's the way it is."*
> "THAT'S THE WAY IT IS," CELINE DION

WHERE DO BELIEFS COME FROM?

Picture one's life as a wave upon the sea, and as one rolls through life, one picks up ideas along the way. Our parents have established and ingrained beliefs in us and so have our teachers, siblings, and friends. Advertisers also influence our belief system. The latest fashion is simply a belief that provides social proof of what is "hot and in style." Thus, because many of us tend to be lazy thinkers, we accept the beliefs that others seek to impose upon us as the "truth."

All of that changes when you *decide* to establish your own beliefs that will carry you to your goals and not away from them. In fact, take a lesson from Oprah Winfrey who said, "You can either see yourself as a wave in the ocean or you can see yourself as the ocean." Start paying attention to which beliefs, thoughts, pictures, and vibrations you are putting into your ocean!

The most important voice to listen to is your own voice that lies within your subconscious and is guided by your light. When you consciously choose to quiet your mind and listen carefully for the inner voice that is your eternal companion, you can truly begin to unlock your purpose; your creativity soars, and the answers to the problems and challenges you face begin to materialize in your day-to-day living. As Dr. Deepak Chopra says, "Get quiet and listen."

LIMITING BELIEFS

"So often times it happens
that we live our lives in chains
and we never even know we have the key."

"ALREADY GONE," THE EAGLES

Every self-help book discusses either directly or indirectly the concept of limiting beliefs. When you think about it, they must. Self-help books seek to replace disempowering beliefs and habits that hold us back in life with empowering beliefs and habits. This book is no different.

The beliefs we hold in our head that are formed over the course of our lifetime and that originate from many sources are driving our behavior and the way we judge others. A belief, as we have seen, is a *feeling* that becomes ingrained in our mind until it directs our behavior. Begin now to explore some of the more common beliefs you hold that are affecting your performance, your view of others, how you are judging yourself, and, most important, how your self-image drives your behavior.

The first limiting belief you need to confront and defeat is the limiting belief that your beliefs "are just the way you are" or "that's the way we always have done it." Remember, we get to choose what our inner voice tells us, and we can instantly change patterns of thinking that have held us back in life.

BELIEFS DON'T HAVE TO MIRROR THE TRUTH

Hopefully the above discussion clarifies that a belief is nothing more than an idea we form in our head regardless of the source it is derived from. A belief may be false or it may be true. Our mind, however, cannot discern between the two because we are not computers—we are bundles of emotional and intellectual energy fields that react to the stimuli (vibrations) around us.

Since our beliefs do not always mirror the truth, and since we get to choose what our inner voice tells us, we have complete control as Jerry and Esther Hicks tell us "to begin to tell a new story." When we place persistent conviction on and instill faith in our new story, soon that new story will begin to materialize. Hence, each of us has the most powerful tool at our disposal: an inner voice that repeatedly communicates to us what we really want in life. Recall the last sentence of chapter 1: "Stick to the things you love, stay committed to your inner truth, and 'the truth shall set you free.'"

If the habitual story you tell yourself every day is derived from your light and consistent with your vision, the "new" story you are telling yourself is indeed the truth. It turns out that any limiting story you have been telling yourself, which has been holding you back, is not the truth after all!

> *"God have mercy on the man*
> *Who doubts what he's sure of."*
>
> "BRILLIANT DISGUISE," BRUCE SPRINGSTEEN

When your story is aligned with your light, it also eliminates another strong force that holds you back—conflicting beliefs. Conflicting beliefs hold us back because they create doubt in our mind. Lack of certainty, in turn, causes fear and procrastination, which hinder our ability to move forward in life—it is the great headwind in life and explains why so many of us take one step forward and two steps back. Here is a simple example of a conflicting belief: "I can tell that girl likes me, but I'm not good enough for her." Your brain has a tough time reconciling how to react to these two beliefs, which are at odds with each other, so it will probably do nothing while it tries to figure out what to do. By then, even if you wanted to ask her out for a date, it may be too late. As Dr. Joe Vitale states, "the Universe likes speed." Your light is the only story you need to tell yourself. Begin to ask for what you want in life and the results will astound you!

MAKE YOUR VOICE YOUR FRIEND

One of the main ways our voice works against us is when we undertake constant "negative self-talk." For me personally, over the years my thoughts gravitated toward habitual derogatory comments about myself: *You dumbass, Typical me, Not again, How can you be so stupid, What a loser I am, I'm jinxed,* and *I'm too nice* or *I'm too soft.* These thoughts evolved over time, and cumulatively, they served only to keep me down. They were not uplifting. This was not the voice that emanated from my light.

Once I began to nurture myself with a voice that empowered me, my life began to change and to head in the direction of my dreams. Over time my voice became my friend, not my foe, and kept me in harmony with my light and my visions. At first, it was difficult to change my habitual pattern of putting myself down. However, once I tapped into my light and once I realized that I alone get to choose my thoughts, good things began to happen for me. The habit itself may have taken some time, but the decision itself to change my habitual negative self-talk took only an instant. Today, my voice habitually speaks to me in clear, reassuring, and exhilarating tones: *You can do it, You rock, Go me,* and *I'm proud of myself.* When I make an error or something does not go my way, I tell myself, *Next play,* like an athlete might after a bad play. Whenever I slip back into my old pattern, I am immediately conscious of it and correct it at once.

Don't let other voices that seek to hold you down in life control you and dictate what your inner voice tells you. From the time we were born, the voices of others—superiors—have told us what to do, what to be, and how to think. As Cat Stevens sang in the song "Father and Son," "From the moment I could talk, I was ordered to listen." The word "no" is the most used word in the English language. It is little wonder, then, that so many of us live our lives following a path that our social consciousness dictates. When you begin to realize that you have an inner voice that comes from Infinite Intelligence, when you begin to identify that voice and listen to it, then you can begin to follow your light and walk the path that is in harmony with who you are—not what the thoughts of others are. Say "yes" to your inner desires! Your light, your vision, and your voice are your three-part harmony in life!

> *"We tend to forget that happiness doesn't come as a result of getting something we don't have, but rather of recognizing and appreciating what we do have."*
> FREDERICK KEONIG, INVENTOR

Use your voice to appreciate and accept who you are and what you want to be. Your voice should encourage you. Pat yourself on the back.

Going easy on yourself does not mean you do not self-reflect or set lower standards than you are capable of or that you let yourself off the hook. It does mean you love yourself and value and cherish your self-worth. You must love yourself and from self-love comes light and strength. If, as you read these words, you are telling yourself that you don't love yourself and you can't love yourself—begin right now to say, "Yes, I can." Think about one time when you laughed or smiled. Think of one instance in your life when you felt self-pride. Allow your light to shine on these moments. You are energy that comes from source. Read on, as chapter 5 will discuss the concept of self-love.

It is easy to be too critical of yourself, and it is equally easy to sell yourself too short. Hold up high standards for yourself—higher than any standards anyone else sets for you. Hold yourself accountable. Those were the standards that Basketball Hall of Famer Julius Erving set for himself. And if there is someone who will encourage you and challenge you to meet your standards, then that is a voice to listen to. Just be sure that the voice reinforces your voice and does not overtake your own voice. And when in doubt, let your light guide you.

Scientists and songwriters tell us that the mind comes in two parts. Part one is your conscious mind, which is also called your objective mind. Your conscious mind is the part of your mind where your thoughts come from. It is the voice within your head. It controls your decision-making and responds to external stimuli. That stimulus can be either negative or positive.

Your subconscious mind is your involuntary thought system. It works automatically twenty-four hours a day, seven days a week, for your entire life. It controls your involuntary muscle and neurological systems like breathing and digestion. When it is fed thoughts from the conscious mind, it begins to work behind the scenes to bring you the things that you hold in your conscious mind. This is where man and the Universe intersect and where magic happens. You can use your voice to dictate to your subconscious mind what you want in life. No one is quite sure how this works exactly, but it does.

As I have already mentioned, too often we listen to other people's voices. Our parents, our friends, our teachers, and our bosses all compete for our inner voice. They want to tell you the story that is "best for you." Because many of us tend to be lazy thinkers, we are easily influenced by outside sources. On the one hand, when you are in tune with your inner voice, you can begin to listen to other voices that support your inner voice. On the other hand, if you find yourself basing decisions on untamed emotions rather than what your inner voice is telling you, it may be time to listen to and evaluate the voices of others. We have all witnessed instances where a friend becomes romantically involved with a person who is a "disaster in waiting." Despite warnings from friends and loved ones, that person does not heed the objective warnings and winds up in a broken and sometimes dangerous relationship. There are times when we need to act rationally despite what our emotions are telling us to focus on.

Examples of voices that empower you are friends, family members, teachers, and consultants who *support* your inner voice and do not try to change your essence. They simply seek to challenge you and bring out the best in you in whatever endeavor you choose. They do not create your path, but they do help you stay on your chosen path and promote your self-growth.

Also, do not underestimate the power of a Mastermind Group. Napoleon Hill, in his inspirational classic

Think and Grow Rich, talks of the mastermind as one of the key steps toward the accumulation of riches. In short, two or more minds produce more and better ideas than one mind can. This explains one of the main reasons why corporations exist and accomplish great feats. It is hard to go it alone, and I can attest to that fact. The key is to join your voice with other voices that are heading in the same direction as your inner voice—even if that other voice is playing devil's advocate with you. That is a voice that is simply helping you focus your light in a positive direction.

For me, my light, my vision, and my voice told me to write this book. This is my book and my creation. However, I have relied upon the input of others to help me craft this book. I have quoted songwriters, scientists, and other great thinkers to reinforce my message. Additionally, I had friends read drafts of this book along the way, and I vetted some of this material during my Toastmaster's speeches. I sought out professional help as well. The point that I am making is that, although my inner voice told me to write this book, I have also relied upon valuable feedback from those who supported my mission to complete this book.

These voices at times challenged me and suggested ways to improve my message, but none of these voices attempted to alter my main themes. The voices I relied upon did not tell me I was wasting my time or I was being fanciful or otherwise discouraged me to complete the book. To the contrary, I was pleasantly surprised by how much encouragement I received in pursuit of my dream. The difference between listening to encouraging voices and discouraging voices can be the dividing line between success, happiness, and harmony in your life.

When you find your voice telling you not to do something because you "don't feel like it," it may be because you are tired, you are fearful, or you are just plain lazy. If you are tired, then rest is in order. I am a big believer in taking life at your own pace. If you are pursuing a worthy cause but fearful of moving forward, then you must, as Dr. Susan Jeffers instructs, "Feel the fear and do it anyway." If you are feeling lazy, then you need to use your voice to tell a better story that will reenergize you. Feel and use your light. Take one step in the right direction and tell yourself that you are making progress. Tony Robbins is fond of saying, "Motion creates emotion."

When you use your voice in an encouraging way, you are feeding your subconscious mind with the nutrients needed to fuel its progress. The subconscious mind will take over and begin to present you with the people, things, and circumstances that will carry you toward fulfillment of your dream.

USE YOUR VOICE TO ENCOURAGE OTHERS

Since we are on the topic of voices, why not use your outer voice to encourage others?

In 2005, I ran the Miami Marathon. It was my second full marathon, but it was the first time I ran a marathon in an all-out attempt to set my own personal record—what runners refer to as a "PR." It was a hot day and a tough race. I remember thinking around mile 16—with still 10 more miles to go—that I might collapse on the pavement, crack my skull, and die right there.

I had never encountered such utter agony before. Still, I struggled on. I slogged through mile after mile, with my legs aching and my head spinning. Miami is run on a flat course with no hills except for the minor inclines from a handful of drawbridges that are part of the course. At about mile 25.5 there was a drawbridge I had to run up before I could make the turn around a corner and head for the finish line, which was less than a mile away.

I was looking at that bridge—the rise could not have been more than 25 feet, but it seemed like Mount Everest in my mind—and telling myself there was no way I could run up that incline. However, as I approached the beginning of the bridge, I heard one voice coming from my left. It was a woman urging me on: *"Come on you can do it, you can do it."* That one single voice—those simple words of encouragement—lifted my spirit and propelled me over that final bridge, and I finished with a new PR of 3:37.

Now more than a dozen years later, I can still hear that voice in my head, and I will remember it forever. I never had and never will have a chance to personally thank that woman, a stranger, except to pay homage to her here. Following her example, I can go forward in my own life and try to never miss an opportunity to encourage others. You may never know what a huge difference it can make in the life of another. Thus, I encourage you to use your voice to encourage others and yourself.

With your light, vision, and voice in harmony with one another, it is now time to get in tune with the power of vibration to attract all the good things that life offers.

Below, you will find examples of common limiting beliefs and empowering beliefs. Identify the limiting beliefs that have been holding you back and resolve to replace your limiting beliefs with those that will empower you!

Examples of Limiting Beliefs	Empowering Beliefs to Replace the Limiting Beliefs
"I don't have the money."	"I have more than enough money." "Thank you, God, for blessing me with health and wealth." "I can find the money." "All I need is within me!" "I can find people with the money and resources I need to get my idea off the ground." "I am rich." "I am wealthy." "I am a money-making machine."
"I'm too old."	"I have lots of experience. Many people older than me have succeeded and so can I." "I am young, powerful, and strong." "I'll never be too old." "I'm young in mind, body, and spirit." "I'm young at heart." "I'm unstoppable."

Examples of Limiting Beliefs	Empowering Beliefs to Replace the Limiting Beliefs
"I'm too young."	"No one is ever too young, especially these days!" "I am young, powerful, and strong." "I'm unstoppable!"
"I'm not smart enough."	"I'm more than smart enough!" "If I can't figure it out for myself, I will find someone who can." "The universe will deliver all the answers that I need."
"I don't have the time."	"I have more than enough time." "Time is on my side, yes it is." "I get to decide how to invest my time." "I have as much time as everyone else." "I'll procrastinate later." "I will schedule the time and commit to the schedule I make for myself."
"He/she won't let me."	"It's my life. No one can stop me from pursuing my dreams!" "I will follow my light at all times." "I am attracting into my life such positive vibrations that nothing and no one can stop me."
"I can't get a break."	"I'm the luckiest person in the world." "Everything is going my way!" "Things are looking up." "I am keeping my chin up." "It's getting better every day."

Examples of Limiting Beliefs	Empowering Beliefs to Replace the Limiting Beliefs
"I'm not healthy enough."	"I'm healthier than a lot of other people." "My health is improving every day and in every way." "I feel great." "I am breathing." "Thank you for my health." "I am blessed with good health." "I am taking control of my nutrition, exercise, and well-being. "I am strong in mind, body, and spirit."
"I'm scared."	"My faith is stronger than my fear." "I won't back down." "I'll face my fear and do it anyway." "I am going to take the first step now."

EXERCISE

➤ Today and forever, be aware of your voice and decide to use it to your advantage. Sit in quiet contemplation. Be alert for your inner voice and listen to it. Use your voice to direct your subconscious to bring to life all the things you want in life. When you do this and use your light, you will uncover the key to success. Tell a new story!

➤ Visualize yourself as the ocean! Then pay attention to the ideas, visions, beliefs, and thoughts you are allowing into the ocean. Focus and deliberately choose what goes into the ocean.

➤ When you are faced with a task you do not feel like doing, determine whether you are tired, lazy, or fearful. If it was one of the latter, use your voice to take one small step toward its completion.

➤ Act on one positive thing your voice tells you to do.

➤ Never miss an opportunity to offer words of encouragement to others.

➤ Pat yourself on the back.

➤ Pick out some empowering beliefs from the list above or create your own. Then, repeat them often to yourself with full emotion so that they are, in fact, empowering you. You may wish to listen to songs that empower you!

➤ Identify one thing you are sure of but doubt anyway. Then act with certainty rather than with doubt in your mind.

➤ As you go through your day, identify one or two limiting beliefs as they arise. What is your inner voice of fear telling you that you can't do? Once you recognize a limiting belief, immediately replace it with an empowering belief regardless of how unnatural it may seem. Repeat your empowering belief at least ten times, and each time put more feeling and belief into it. For example, Limiting Belief: "I don't have enough time to write a book." Empowering Belief: "I have more than enough time to write a book—I get to choose how I spend my time and lots of busy people write books. I can, I must, and I am."

"Like your oldest friend,
just trust the voice within
Then you'll find the strength
that will guide your way"
"THE VOICE WITHIN," CHRISTINA AGUILERA

CHAPTER FOUR

THE VIBE

"I'm picking up good vibrations . . .
good, good, good, good vibrations."
"GOOD VIBRATIONS," THE BEACH BOYS

EVERYTHING MOVES, AND EVERYTHING THAT MOVES moves all the time. The Universe is made up of one substance, the God Particle, and this substance is not stagnant. Instead, it vibrates all the time. The Universe itself is vibrating. Scientists can now discern through highly powered microscopes that even inanimate objects like a chair are made up of vibrating atoms, and thus, everything is moving on the inside. No wonder the power of music is really the power of vibration. Your ability to remain in motion and your ability to head in the right direction determine your future. You can do this by using what has come to be known as the law of attraction.

In *Think and Grow Rich*, Napoleon Hill described the law of attraction (without calling it that) in chapter 3, "Faith," as follows:

The human mind is constantly attracting vibrations which harmonize with that which DOMINATES the human mind. Any thought, idea, plan, or purpose which one *holds* in one's mind attracts, from the vibrations of the ether, a host of its relatives, adds these "relatives" to its own force, and grows until it becomes the dominating, MOTIVATING MASTER of the individual in whose mind it has been housed.

While everything is internally vibrating and therefore changing, everything is moving externally as well. The elements of wind, rain, fire, and solar energy keep things in a constant state of flux. These elements change the very fabric of objects, both living and inanimate. For example, a continuous drip of water on the hardest stone will eventually wear down the stone—even if it takes thousands of years. We, as humans, are nothing more than vibrational forces of energy living and interacting amidst other vibrating forces of energy. When we add magnetic force to the equation, we can begin to unlock the mystery of the Universe. It's called the law of attraction. We are constantly attracting people, things, and places to us, and people, things, and places are attracting us to them. Our dominating impulses of thought are magnetic forces that bring to us what it is that we dwell upon the most.

The purpose of this book is not to immerse you in the law of attraction. It is intended to illustrate, though, the power that the law of attraction has upon our individual life story. Thus, you are encouraged to act upon the faith that the law of attraction is one of the great laws of the Universe, just as Newton introduced us to the law of gravity. We don't need to know how gravity works to put it to good use in our everyday lives. Similarly, the mere acceptance of the law of attraction—i.e., that we attract to us what we intend to attract—is all we need to effectively implement it into our lives. When viewed in this vein, we begin to see why an inner light, voice, and vision, as discussed in the first three chapters, are so vital to our direction in life.

Since you are a vibrational force, use your voice and make it a point to entertain good vibrations. If you want to delve deeper into the law of attraction, read *The Secret* by Rhonda Byrne; *Money, and the Law of Attraction: Learning to Attract Wealth, Health, and Happiness* by Jerry and Esther Hicks; and *The Attractor Factor: 5 Easy Steps for Creating Wealth (or Anything Else) from the Inside Out* by Joe Vitale. And, if you really wish to go deep into the concept, read Emerson and Thoreau.

One of my favorite quotes as it relates to the law of attraction comes from Jim Rohn. He said, "Success is not something you pursue. What you pursue will elude you. It can be like trying to chase butterflies. Success is something you attract and accumulate by the person you become." The reason this quote resonates with me so much is that many gloss over the point that the stronger our magnetic pull the more we can attract the very things we want into our lives. Rohn's quote places the emphasis on personal development and self-growth, which is the very point of our existence. When you use your light, you become an instant success because your positive energy and good vibrations will create a magnetic radiance about you that will begin to attract to you the people, places, things, and circumstances into your life you most deserve and desire. It does not so much matter where you start from; you just need to start throwing off positive energy, which will move you in the right general direction.

I was once speaking to a class of college students who were seeking their degree in paralegal studies. Many were bemoaning the age-old paradox of "How do you get experience if you can't get a job, but how do you get a job without experience?" The answer, I told them, is easy. Begin with where you are and with what you have. I explained to the students that there is no shame in beginning your legal career as a file clerk in a law firm if that is the best job you can start with. Accepting an entry-level position puts you in the game. Once you are in the game, you are in the stream of commerce and you can advance your career by improving yourself. You will begin to attract things into your life—networking contacts, job references, experience, etc. You are in the game, and you are gaining valuable experience and valuable relationships.

To demonstrate my point, I used an extreme example. If LeBron James started as a ball boy for a team, say, in Europe, is there any doubt that his talent and desire would have still carried him to the top of the basketball world? True, it may have taken him longer to get to the top of the basketball world, but as long as he held the desire to be the best, his success was inevitable.

If you are starting from the bottom, know that as long as you hold off discouragement and instead focus on progress and improvement, you will succeed! Do not make excuses—make progress instead! This is not to say that the farther up the road you start the better,

for the farther up the road you start, the more bene-
ficial it will be for you. However, as long as you focus
on becoming an attractive person through faith and
self-development, in the end, it will not matter. Invest
the time and thought required to increase the strength
of your vibrational magnetic force through personal
self-development. You will get further quicker if you
simply get into the stream of commerce—as long as you
remain alert for what you want and are willing to go
with your vibrational flow. Don't stay on the sidelines
your whole life waiting for a moment that may never
come. Keep moving!

POSITIVE ENERGY/POSITIVE LIFE/ POSITIVE RESULT

Tony Robbins often states that he does not believe in
positive thinking. He uses a strong analogy to demonstrate his point. If you see weeds in the garden and then
just stand there and think positive thoughts but take
no action, the weeds will remain in the garden. To be
fair, he does not believe in negativity either. Rather, he
advocates for seeing things the way they are, no better
or worse than they really are.

I think Robbins mostly has it right, and, yet, while I
am all for simplicity, his analogy sounds a bit too sim-
plistic to me. This book, after all, is about living with
passion and ruling it with reason. To be sure, there are
plenty of examples where the very vibrational thought
of pulling weeds can send out a signal to other forces
that make the weeds vanish. For example, on the morning of my son Austin's high school graduation, I was

tidying up our house for the postgraduation party. I noticed that there were weeds in one of our garden beds. I did not have enough time to pull them myself, but thought, *Wouldn't it be nice if the weeds were gone?* About twenty minutes later, the gardener who cuts our hedges came by, and I took the opportunity to ask if I could pay him to pull the weeds in addition to cutting the hedges. *Whoosh!* The weeds were gone. The very thought of the weeds being gone created focus in my universe and *wham* it was done. However, notice that even though I did not physically pull the weeds myself, I did take action. I identified a person in the Universe who could help me, asked him to weed the garden bed, and then paid him a fair wage for his services.

Thus, returning to Robbins's analogy, I agree that mere positive thought without any follow-up action rarely will produce the specific response you seek. Man has not yet progressed to the apex of development where a simple thought automatically produces a specified result. By this I mean that the lottery winner still had to buy the ticket or accept it as a gift from someone. However, the action you take may be something other than yanking out the weeds by yourself. By simply focusing your attention and remaining alert for the opportunity, you will inevitably create good vibrations that produce a person, place, situation, or thing that can aid in your manifestation. In fact, your reluctance to act may lead to a breakthrough. It is said that some of the laziest people come up with the greatest inventions. Why? They look for the easiest way to accomplish a task. The advent of weed killers and weedwackers to make the job easier are examples of this. That is called progress through the thought of man, and there is nothing wrong with that. Indeed, it is good.

In chapter 3 of *Think and Grow Rich*, Napoleon Hill talks about the benefits of positivity: "A mind dominated by positive emotions becomes a favorable abode for the state of mind known as faith. A mind so dominated may, at will, give the subconscious mind instructions, which it will accept and act upon immediately."

Scientific research continues to uncover the fact that positive thinking and emotions are good for both short-term and long-term well-being. In Professor Barbara L. Fredrickson's paper, "The Role of Positive Emotions in Positive Psychology: The Broaden-and-Build Theory of Positive Emotions," she examined the scientific studies surrounding the study of positive thinking, and concluded:

> The broaden-and-build theory underscores the ways in which positive emotions are essential elements of optimal functioning, and therefore an essential topic within the science of well-being. The theory, together with the research reviewed here, suggests that positive emotions: (i) broaden people's attention and thinking; (ii) undo lingering negative emotional arousal; (iii) fuel psychological resilience; (iv) build consequential personal resources; (v) trigger upward spirals towards greater well-being in the future; and (vi) seed human flourishing. The theory also carries an important prescriptive message. People should cultivate positive emotions in their own lives and in the lives of those around them, not just because doing so makes them feel good in the moment, but also because doing so transforms

people for the better and sets them on paths toward flourishing and healthy longevity. When positive emotions are in short supply, people get stuck. They lose their degrees of behavioral freedom and become painfully predictable. But when positive emotions are in ample supply, people take off. They become generative, creative, resilient, ripe with possibility, and beautifully complex. The broaden-and-build theory conveys how positive emotions move people forward and lift them to the higher ground of optimal well-being.[5]

Begin focusing on viewing things from a positive perspective. Carry a positive mental attitude and approach to all your endeavors. Treat others with a positive feeling of camaraderie. This especially applies to your foes. Remember, we cannot fully judge others unless we have walked in their moccasins. Focus on their good traits and watch how your so-called enemy reciprocates. Feel the good vibrations you are sending out with each positive thought. Pay attention to how your good vibrations create positive energy and attract positive things into your life.

Norman Vincent Peale said this: "Our happiness depends on the habit of mind we cultivate. So practice happy thinking every day. Cultivate the merry heart, develop the happiness habit, and life will become a continual feast."

I MUST, I CAN, AND I AM

The main difference between people who "make it" and those who fall short of their goals boils down to one thing: *definite decision-making*. When we make a definite decision on a desired outcome and then remain alert toward its fulfillment, we embrace personal power. When we *fully decide and commit* to do something, become something, or get something, we become proactive rather than reactive. And when we become proactive, things begin to happen for us—and not to us. Dedicate yourself to your purpose and start acting (however small or large the act) toward its fulfillment.

In other words, achievers do not simply sit back and wait for conditions to be just right before embarking upon their journey. Instead, they take action from where they stand and their action is backed by thought and faith. In turn, the positive vibrational forces of the Universe begin to arrange themselves and conform to the person's desires. This is the real magic and explanation of the law of attraction. When a leader makes a definitive decision to head in a certain direction, then his or her people, resources, and energy join together and they move in unison toward the organization's goal. The process gains momentum and soon everything within its sphere is swept up like a tornado, pulling up all objects in its path. Learn to *act* and not simply *react* to situations and soon life will begin to take the shape you want it to take. Remember, live your life on the balls of your feet.

Since the impetus of manifestation starts with a definite decision, it must follow that good decisions lead you toward good results, and poor decisions gravitate toward poor results. The adage "garbage in, garbage out" is very pertinent when it comes to decision-making. As Les Brown says, "Do what you know and not what you feel." Remember, Dr. Albert Schweitzer says *thinking* is the hardest thing you will ever be called upon to do.

If you want to change your life starting this very instant, you can. It all starts with one good decision at a time. Start with something easy so you can gain focus, momentum, confidence, power, and faith. For example, choose to give up drinking alcohol for one day, make good eating decisions, put five dollars away, or make the call you have been putting off. When you do, you will begin to head in the right direction. It does not matter where you begin. Many lottery winners or those who inherit a lot of money lose their money through poor decision-making, while the vast majority of the world's wealthiest people as listed yearly by Forbes created their own wealth.

What is the difference between good decisions and bad decisions? To begin with, good decisions are not always easy decisions, but they are not always that hard to make either. It is not too difficult to recognize that poor diet and exercise habits will likely lead to poor health over the long run, but committing to the decision to change and then sticking with it is often the hard part. One way to identify a good decision is when it aligns with your purpose and your values. Another way to view decisions is to think about the time or money they will cost you. Are you *spending* time and money, or are you *investing* time and money? Investing time and energy today can go a long way toward having what you want tomorrow. As Zig Ziglar often stated, "When you do the things you need to do, when you need to do them, the day will come when you can do the things you want to do, when you want to do them." Do the right thing now!

Once you make a good decision, you then must remain committed to exercising that decision. "Do or do not, there is no try," said Yoda. No one will write your bucket list for you, no one will write my book for me, and no one will give up anything until they decide to do so. You may want to lose weight and you may forever be searching for the perfect diet, but until you really commit to losing weight and see yourself losing weight, you won't realize permanent weight loss. In other words, make the "big decision" to lose weight. Then as you go through the day, you need to make one good "little decision" at a time by eating or not eating what will bring your closer to your goal. If you want to increase your likelihood of succeeding, then plan—have the right foods in front of you when it is time to eat. Weight loss, like everything else in the human experience—including happiness—is an inside job. Here is where you can use the vibrational forces of the Universe and direct your inner light, vision, and voice to adopt what I call a "I must, I can, and I am" attitude.

I Must

Usually, you need a big enough reason to either start something new or to quit doing something that is detrimental to your well-being. There is a great scene in the movie *Cinderella Man*, a true-life story of the improbable comeback of a broke, underdog, and scrappy fighter, Jim Braddock, during the depression era. At a press conference, a reporter asked him what the biggest difference was between his losses and wins. His answer was prophetic: "I figured out what I was fighting for." In his case, it was to feed his family and keep them together. That one reason was so powerful that it was strong enough to propel him to beat many bigger, stronger, younger, and faster opponents, including the ferocious Max Baer. He viewed himself as a champion because he had to be a champion if he was going to be able to keep his family together. Similarly, the person who has a heart attack at an early age after decades of poor habits receives their wake-up call and changes their diet, exercise, and outlook on life. Instead of dying, they begin to live life to the fullest by transforming into a healthy, happy, and fulfilled person.

View yourself as a winner and then start behaving like one. If you want to be a Division I athlete, you must behave like a Division I athlete, which takes dedication, practice, and perseverance. My daughter Megan viewed herself in this vein, dedicated herself to mastering the sport of lacrosse, and fulfilled her dream of playing Division I lacrosse. Whatever your craft or cause is, dedicate yourself toward mastering it.

Prophetic change does not have to be that hard a decision. When I sign up and pay a fee to run a marathon, I am now committed and I stick to my plan. When I have no such race in sight, my training drifts. Choose an area in your life that needs improvement. Come up with a big enough reason as to why the change is worth it—an "I must" reason will be infinitely more powerful than an "I should" reason, and you have just completed one-third of your goal.

We all want to increase our income. There is a natural

inclination toward growth in the human experience. The Bible does not forbid us to be wealthy as long as it is reaped from just pursuits: "Honour the LORD with thy substance, and with the firstfruits of all thine increase: So shall thy barns be filled with plenty, and thy presses shall burst out with new wine" (Proverbs 3:9-10, KJV). Pick one reason why you must commit to increasing wealth and you are well on your way to its achievement.

I Can

What seems the hardest part of the journey to success is perhaps the easiest. Even when we have an "I must" reason, it is easy to become overwhelmed and confused with *how* we can achieve our goals. When you run a marathon, the course is laid out for you. There is a specific start time, starting line, and finish line. The signs along the course tell you where to go. In life, though, you have to find your own path since there is not always a specific course laid out for you. Here are a few thoughts on how to overcome this prong of the success formula.

First, the easiest way to gain guidance is to model the paths of others. There are millions of books on dieting, finance, and success. We live in an information era, and the internet is chock-full of resources that point you to the ways and means in which to accomplish virtually any task you set your mind to. Thus, you can begin to marshal the information that will help you chart a path toward fulfillment of your desired object. You can also hire a coach or team up with a friend who is dedicated to the same goal you have.

Second, don't underestimate the power of experience. If you want to get good at something, you must practice it. Reading a book on golf can provide you with valuable swing techniques, but you must get out and play. You must practice and adjust accordingly to improve yourself. This also goes back to my advice to the paralegal students. By accepting an entry-level job in a law firm, you are instantly gaining experience. You are associating with people who have knowledge that can be imparted to you. A simple distinction here and a fine distinction there can suddenly open new paths for you.

Third, you don't have to go it alone. You can attract others around you simply by setting your intention toward your desired outcome. It may be helpful for you to know that Andrew Carnegie knew very little about the production of steel when he built his steel empire. Instead, he organized world-class talent around him and attracted the people who were experts in the production of steel and industry. And, yes, he understood the law of attraction, and he practiced unwavering faith with focus in a positive frame of mind. Apply faith with focus in your life and see where it may take you.

Fourth, and many of us never take the time to do this, but we must take the time to analyze our results. Whatever it is you are trying to accomplish, you simply must pay attention to whether your activity is working or not. You can do this by remaining alert for what is working and by establishing metrics in which to track your progress. If you are a salesperson, are you making enough calls? Are you reaching the right decision-maker? Are you engaging your prospect with a planned-out approach? How is your closing ratio? Once you get on top of your numbers, you can begin to convert the art of the sale into the science of success. Notice that the process of analysis does not require great physical activity, but it does require deep and sustained thought. Like everything else, the more you engage in deep thought, the better you will get at it.

I Am

> *"Livin' in the moment,*
> *I'm livin' in the moment.*
> *You bet your ass I own it,*
> *I'm livin' in the moment."*

"LIVIN' IN THE MOMENT," AUSTIN JAMES

Begin right now to focus on the person you want to be, the things you want to do, and the things you want to have. See and feel yourself already in possession of what you want, act as if you are the person you want to be, and see yourself doing the things you want to do. Then make one good decision and act upon it. Stop telling yourself, "I will," and start telling yourself, "I am." Start living in the moment and watch as the vibration of the Universe begins to arrange things for you. Your faith with focused determination will begin to make things happen for you and not to you. By telling yourself, "I am," you will begin to form a new identity of a doer and not a bystander.

Faith with focus backed by determination and perseverance will equal success. That is the success formula. Because this is a book about faith with focus, I add that asking the general Universe for something is a good start. For example, if you want a million dollars, ask the Universe to deliver it to you. But then focus on asking specific people in the Universe for an order if you are in sales or financing or for a partnership. Maybe you need the record producer or agent or publishing house to say yes to you. Identify the right people and ask them "early and often" what it is you want, and watch the magic unfold. This works in your personal life as well. If you want to attract the right person into your life, start off by asking the Universe for your ideal mate, but then be on the lookout for that person you can ask out for a date or establish a relationship with.

Is this going to be your shining, breakthrough moment? Is this the moment in time and space where you choose and commit to your chosen destiny? If it feels right, if it makes sense, and it is within God's purview, determine to set about your course right this instant. Do not put off this decision another second. Act (do not react) now. All your successes, achievements, and happiness will be traced back to that one moment with just one good decision you made to move in the direction you wish to travel. Your life will never be the same. After completing the following exercises, turn the page and you will uncover the greatest gift of all.

EXERCISE

➤ Backed by the strength of your "I must, I can, and I am" attitude, choose one task you have been putting off and do it today. If there is a phone call you need to make, make it. If someone is waiting on an answer for a commitment from you, make a good decision and either commit or decline. Whatever it is that you have been putting off, resolve to take care of it today.

➤ Use your light to focus on and feel the good vibrations.

➤ Ask the Universe for something you want. Then ask a specific person in the Universe for the same thing.

➤ Make one "big decision" like losing weight. Then as you go through your day, make one good "little decision" at a time to support your big decision, such as eating the right food that supports your weight-loss goal.

➤ Stay alert for the outside circumstances that are being drawn to your good vibrations.

➤ Engage in personal self-development to become "an attractive person."

➤ **Extra Credit:** Listen to the song "Good Vibrations" by the Beach Boys.

*"Welcome to the new age, to the new age
Whoa, oh, oh, oh, oh, whoa, oh, oh, oh,
I'm radioactive, radioactive."*

"RADIOACTIVE," IMAGINE DRAGONS

CHAPTER FIVE

THE GREATEST LOVE OF ALL

"Learning to love yourself
It is the greatest love of all."

"GREATEST LOVE OF ALL," WHITNEY HOUSTON

AT THE END OF THE DAY, IT DOESN'T REALLY MATTER if you are rich or poor. What matters most is that you live a fulfilling and happy life. It is hard to imagine someone who truly loves himself or herself for who they are (not for what they have achieved) and not be happy or fulfilled. Conversely, it is hard to imagine someone being truly happy no matter how much outer success they have if they do not love themselves. Tragically and ironically, Whitney Houston and her daughter, Bobbi Kristina Brown, presumably did not show the self-love necessary to prohibit self-destruction by using drugs.

Notwithstanding, the greatest part of this "don't worry, be happy" (Bobby McFerrin) success formula is that you can choose to love yourself. It is the best gift you will ever give to yourself. Go back to the last exercise in chapter 4 and make the single-best decision you will ever make in your lifetime—decide right now that you love yourself, really, really love yourself. Why shouldn't you? Give yourself the gift of self-love, and you will suddenly find it easy to accept all the other gifts the Universe has in store for you: money, success, freedom, peace, and even fame if you want it. It will no longer be awkward for you when someone gives you a gift or showers you with praise. When money unexpectedly comes into your life, you will know that you are deserving of it. You are also deserving of the "love of your life" being part of your life. Be grateful for who you are, where you are, and what you have. Willie Nelson has said that once he started counting his blessings, his whole life changed. That is a powerful statement to abide by.

You can decide to love yourself. Commit yourself *right now* to mastering self-love and getting hooked on it. Throw away any self-defeating images you may have had about yourself up until now. In fact, choose one self-image that has been holding you back. For me, one of the self-images that holds me back at times is the image that I have of myself trying to please others all the time. This is not necessarily a bad thing except when I unnecessarily elevate other people's needs ahead of my own. At times, this prohibits me from taking the initiative to make sure I work on the pursuit of my own dreams. It is easier for me to provide service to others because it allows me to avoid the uncertainty of the risk that chasing my own dreams invokes.

Once you have selected a negative self-image, undertake the following exercise that I learned by listening to Dr. Wayne Dyer. First, thank the negative image for everything it has done for you up to now. Do not get angry or be mad at it. Indeed, the image you are thinking about has protected you, and it has served you well. It has allowed you to shelter yourself, and it has probably earned you attention from others. Tell that image that you love it for it has always been there for you.

After expressing your gratitude and love for this image, it is now time to say good-bye and let this image go from your mind. This negative image of yours must go. The self-doubting, self-pitying, and self-defeating image of yourself must part ways with you. Decide to replace it with a new image of yourself, a new concept. There is a new limitless, fearless, and determined you that is choosing to act, choosing to have things happen for you and not to you that is stepping out. Start living your life on the balls of your feet—especially when you are confronted with a challenging situation like a diffi-cult conversation you must have with someone. You are letting your love shine, and it feels amazing!

To me, the most interesting aspect of the Whit-ney Houston lyric, written by Linda Creed after being diagnosed with cancer, are the words "learning to love yourself." Think about it. It was God's choice that we were born of this world. Our birth is not an accident any more than the shinbone being connected to the knee bone is an accident. We are a part of the Universal order, and we come from the God Particle. Therefore, why wouldn't we love ourselves? When we were born, we naturally loved ourselves. We were not born hating ourselves or depriving ourselves. What happened then? If you struggle with self-love, when did you begin to deprive yourself of your own self-worth? And why must you now begin to relearn how to love yourself?

My suspicion is that as we grew older and began to mature, we started to listen more to the voices of others. We lost awareness of our own inner light and voice and no longer relied upon our own thinking to guide us toward our true purpose. When parents told us we were "bad," we listened to them rather than listening to our own voice telling us that we weren't bad. We believed teachers who told us we were "dumb" even though we weren't. We ignored our own special talents because we listened to others tell us what we were and what we were not. Slowly, over time, our own voice started telling us the same things others were telling us. Their voice became our voice, and we lost our innate voice, our light, and our vision, and our own self-worth diminished. We stopped loving and honoring ourselves. (As an aside, going forward, be careful not to criticize anyone. The slightest comment upon someone's physical appearance, for example, can truly crush a person.)

Jesus taught us the Golden Rule: "Do unto others as you would have them do unto you." Until recently, I have always interpreted this principle to mean to treat others well at a cost to myself. I still strongly subscribe to the populist interpretation to help others, for studies reveal that this is where the greatest human fulfillment occurs. Personally, I find great joy in helping others. However, as I have become more aware of my own light, I have come to recognize the underlying message of the words of Jesus—*it starts with the premise that we love ourselves first.* Jesus does not tell us to do better for others than we would do for ourselves. Instead, he says to do the same for others that we would do for ourselves. This is Jesus's message. Love yourself and love others equally. We can't maximize our contribution to others until we first do well unto ourselves. Treat others well and treat yourself well, too. Hence, be kind, loving, compassionate, and respectful to yourself.

How do we love ourselves throughout the course of our day? Here are some ideas. We love ourselves so much that we make the time to exercise on a regular basis. We love ourselves so much that we are mindful of our nutritional choices. We do not totally deprive ourselves for that is not really self-love, but we remain moderate. We don't overdo it with alcohol. We love ourselves too much for that. We listen to our voice, and we follow our light. We allow our hidden talents to shine through. If we love to read, we read. If our inner voice is telling us to go to the beach, we honor that voice and go to the beach. We also follow our passion and we find our purpose. Heed the words of John A. Shedd, who said, "A ship in harbor is safe, but that is not what ships are built for."

Is all this talk of self-love just a code for preaching selfishness? To some extent, yes. Loving yourself does not mean to be so vain and so self-serving that we ignore helping others. For in the end, helping others makes us feel good. It gives our lives meaning and purpose. However, it does not mean we ignore our own needs and desires either. We do unto ourselves as we do unto others. If you are a great friend to others, then be a great friend to yourself. If you are a "go giver" to others, be a "go giver" to yourself. If you help others dreams come true, then make your own dreams come true. When our dreams come true, we are actually in a better position to help more people make their dreams come true. For example, if you tithe 10 percent of your income to the church, then you can readily see that 10 percent of a million is $100,000, which is a lot more than 10 percent of, say, $30,000. Get the point?

> *"Some people claim*
> *That there's a woman to blame,*
> *But I know, it's my own damn fault."*
> "MARGARITAVILLE," JIMMY BUFFETT

If you are going to truly love yourself, you must be willing to take responsibility for your life. This means taking responsibility for everything that happens to you in life *even if it is not your fault!* When something bad happens to you through no fault of your own, it is still your responsibility to deal with it. When you break out of a victim-mode mentality, you begin to develop the inner grit that propels you toward accomplishment. Be a victor, not a victim! I used to tell my children whenever they would whine about a "bad teacher" or an "unfair test" that they were still responsible to do their best and receive the best grade they could get. Think about it: 2 + 2 = 4 no matter how hard the teacher may be. After all, it is their grade that shows up on the report card and that college admissions committees look at—without giving consideration to who one's teachers were.

Most of us have had difficult bosses at one point. My father-in-law had such a boss early in his career while he was rising through the ranks in higher education. As an assistant dean at a major university, he spent three years accepting difficult assignment after difficult assignment and never once received a compliment from the dean. There was much negativity in the department as the dean epitomized the term "sourpuss." While others complained, my father-in-law kept working hard and tackled every assignment given to him with full vigor. When my father-in-law resigned after a few years to accept a higher-ranking job at another university, the dean pulled him aside and said, "Phil, I just want to thank you for your service. You were the only person in my department that I could count on." Is it any wonder, then, that my-father-in-law, born to uneducated Italian immigrants during the depression era, rose to become a college president?

When you accept responsibility for *everything* in your life, you take control of your life. This is where your personal power comes from. This is where your inner faith springs forth, and this is where you gain courage. Behave like a victor and not a victim of circumstances, and watch as your faith, self-image, and self-respect flourish.

With the impetus of self-love, you can now begin to honor your dreams. However, before turning the page, complete the following exercises.

EXERCISE

➢ Look for the good in yourself and focus on it. Bruno Mars says, "You're amazing, just the way you are."

➢ Look at yourself in the mirror and tell yourself, "I love you, I love you using your name. I really, really, really love you."

➢ Live your life with an attitude of gratitude and count your blessings.

➢ Starting now, love and honor yourself so that you:

  ▶ Choose to go to bed early so you can get a good night's sleep.

  ▶ Wake up early after a good night's sleep with a jovial expectation that a successful day awaits: "This is the day that the Lord has made."

  ▶ Choose to exercise and make sensible dieting decisions.

  ▶ Choose to work on self-development.

  ▶ Establish your priorities and stick to them.

  ▶ Work on making your dreams come true.

  ▶ Do something fun.

  ▶ Identify a negative self-image that has been holding you down. Acknowledge it, thank it for the protection it has afforded you up until now, and then say good-bye to it. Replace it with an uplifting belief.

- ➤ Determine the value of your services and then ask for what you're worth.

- ➤ Get quiet and listen.

- ➤ Take one action right now toward the fulfillment of your dreams.

- ➤ Take responsibility for everything that occurs in your life.

- ➤ Behave like a victor and not a victim.

- ➤ Visualize your ship sailing out of the harbor to the ocean of your dreams.

"You're simply the best,
better than all the rest
Better than anyone,
anyone I ever met."
"THE BEST," TINA TURNER

"I am beautiful
In every single way."
"BEAUTIFUL," CHRISTINA AGUILERA

CHAPTER SIX

THE DREAM

"Dream on, Dream on,
Dream until your dreams come true."

"DREAM ON," AEROSMITH

WE HAVE COME TO THE POINT OF THE BOOK where we can apply what we have learned about the substance of faith and its characteristics that begin to bring it into focus. By now, you have built up enough faith within you to know that all things are, indeed, possible. You know that your life's purpose is to follow your inner light—especially when the outside circumstances around you are dark. You now know you are worthy of expecting and receiving the best that life has to offer. You also know there is a greater unifying force than yourself that connects all things together through one substance. Through Universal vibrations, you are attracting the things in your life that you are seeing in your head, feeling in your body, and what your inner voice is telling you. You now know and have the power to begin manifesting the things in life that matter the most to you. In short, you are ready to have the things you really want. Let's get started, then, to bring to you all the good things in life that are meant for you.

All great achievements start with a dream. And not just any dream, but a big dream—a dream so big that the very thought of it makes your toes tingle and your heart flutter. It makes your light shine, puts you on the balls of your feet, smile, and love yourself. You can see it; you can feel it. You can hear it inside your head. You dwell upon this dream so much that after a while it is no longer a dream—it is your reality because as you feel it, it becomes you. It may be the multimillion-dollar enterprise you created, the big mansion, the fancy car, your soul mate, the mended relationship, the book you wrote, the song you sang in concert, the cure to your illness, or the marathon you ran. It may be all of the above.

The point is we are all dreamers! The problem with most of us is that we abandon our dreams much too early to give them a fighting chance of coming true. We get caught up in other things—the grind of day-to-day living just to survive. Most of us are conditioned at an early age not to dream too big, not to dare too much, and not to expect the best. Other people have better plans in mind for us. So it goes and so it seems that dreams are for others to reach, but not for our dream to come true.

*"To accomplish great things,
we must not only act,
but also dream; not only plan,
but also believe."*

ANATOLE FRANCE

I am here to tell you that "life is but a dream," and you are living it right now. This is one exercise that can't wait until the end of this chapter to complete. Stop right now and think of a dream that is so big that it knocks your socks off. What is your greatest *passion* in life? What do you want your dream life to look like? Where is your light leading you? What is it that you desire the most? Are you discovering your life's purpose?

Go back to your childhood. Was there one dream you had? When did you give up on it? Why? Is there someone in your life you think of and say to yourself, "I wish I was like him or her?" This is the dream you are going to manifest starting right now. This will be your focus from here on out. You will begin with the end in mind and then start at once to head in its general direction. Impossible? Not at all. How do you think the great artists I have been quoting pulled it off? They had a dream, and they moved in the direction of their dream. They took action, and that action went from their inner mind to the outer Universe. They acted and let the Universe react to them. You can, you must, and you are going to do the same thing starting this instant. Get passionate!

Wait a second, you say. Isn't this a book about living your life with reason as well as having faith? Aren't I a little too old to make it on the PGA or LPGA Tour? Well, yes and no. Your main mission in life is to follow your light toward happiness and fulfillment. The whole idea is to pick out something you love to do and then figure out how to make a living at it.

Bestselling author Mike Dooley often speaks about focusing only upon the outcome and not concerning yourself with what he labels the "cursed hows." For example, let's say you want a Mercedes Benz, and every day you spend five minutes visualizing yourself in your brand-new Mercedes tooling down the highway. As you hold that thought in your mind, you begin to attract events, so that through the magic of metaphysics, you end up with a 750 series BMW fully loaded instead. The end result is the same—you are still happy and rocking your brand-new car. In other words, set your sights on the end result, but do not attach to it.

Returning to the PGA tour dream, maybe you won't make it as a player on the PGA or LPGA, but maybe you will be a caddie, a golf merchandiser, or an executive with the PGA. Perhaps you will start a business that provides a product or service that pro golfers demand. Maybe you will start doing many business deals on the golf course, so, in a way, you are getting paid to play golf! You get the point.

For me, I have always loved music, and when I was a kid, I used to pretend I was in a rock-and-roll band. It never did get past the "pretend" stage for me, but I did write song lyrics during high school classes. I had to write a poem for my English class, and my English teacher was impressed and told me that "this is a real poem." Had I known then what I know now about the law of attraction, I may have pushed songwriting to a new level.

Nonetheless, fast-forward thirty-five years later, and I have cowritten a published song with an award-winning songwriter, and now I am writing this book laden with lyrics. This stuff works. Had I been more knowledgeable back then perhaps I could have sped up the timing of things, but then again, I would have missed out on my life experiences that brought me to this point.

As for the "impossibility" argument—vanish it from your mind. If you asked the average person a hundred and fifty years ago whether it would be possible to communicate by fax, email, and phone, they would have called you crazy. As noted before, the human mind has not evolved yet to the point that all manifestation of any thought is immediately ascertainable, but do not underestimate the power of the human mind and spirit. Imagine the advances there will be over the next one hundred years—all of which will come from man's creative vision, thought, faith, and, of course, focus.

How specific should your dream be? Mike Dooley imagined a dream life filled with abundance, international travel, a perfect relationship, and creative and fulfilling work. That is a list that I suspect works for most of us. He did not get more specific than that, but he began at once to move in the general direction of the life he imagined. He joined Toastmasters, spoke for free at Rotary Club meetings, and kept knocking on more doors.

Eventually, all of his past experiences that theretofore may have been labeled "failures" began to present themselves as pieces of one puzzle. The sum of his experiences resulted in a dream life as a highly successful, materially abundant, and creative international speaker. Along his journey he met his wife, and now Mike is a dad to boot!

*"I learned this, at least, by my experiment;
that if one advances confidently
in the direction of his dreams, and
endeavors to live the life which he has
imagined, he will meet with a success
unexpected in common hours."*[6]

HENRY DAVID THOREAU

Heed the words of Thoreau. Get on the balls of your feet. Follow your light with confidence and start heading in the general direction of your dreams, the life you have imagined, and see how far it will take you! By now, you should have the confidence to do so. If you are wondering if you can pull it off, then draw inspiration from the words of spiritual activist, author, and lecturer Marianne Williamson, as she says in a quote often misattributed to Nelson Mandela:

Our deepest fear is not that we are inadequate. Our deepest fear is that we are powerful beyond measure. It is our light, not our darkness, that most frightens us. We ask ourselves, Who am I to be brilliant, gorgeous, talented, and fabulous? Actually, who are you not to be? You are a child of God. Your playing small does not serve the world. There is nothing enlightened about shrinking so that other people will not feel insecure around you. We are all meant to shine, as children do. We were born to make manifest the glory of God that is within us. It is not just in some of us; it is in everyone and as we let our own light shine, we unconsciously give others permission to do the same. As we are liberated from our own fear, our presence automatically liberates others.[7]

In the next chapter, we will begin to establish goals that support the dream we have identified for ourselves so that we can begin to use physical activity and the power of thought to move in the direction of the dreams we have imagined for ourselves. We will choose goals that allow us to enjoy the journey! Setting written goals is an important stepping-stone for dream manifestation. However, before we set those goals, let's take some time to identify the underlying reasons for our dreams, and let's be sure that we set goals that truly excite and inspire us.

EXERCISE

➤ What does your dream life look like? Write it down. Read and speak out loud your dream at least twice per day. (Don't skip this step!)

➤ Take one action toward the fulfillment of your dream. It can be as simple as looking up the cost of your oceanfront property. Do it now!

➤ Return to your dream and spend at least five minutes visualizing its realization each day.

➤ Consider making a vision board to keep your dream life visible to you often.

➤ Pretend that you are celebrating the fulfillment of your dream as if it just happened. For example, how would you feel and how would you move around if you just discovered you won the lottery? Jump around, hoot and holler, feel the feeling, and see the vision!

➤ Now, hold on to that feeling. In the next chapter, you will begin to set goals toward fulfilling your dream.

➤ What do you want to create? What will your legacy be? Decide right now and the ensuing chapters will guide you toward its realization.

"Don't stop believin'
Hold on to that feelin'."

"DON'T STOP BELIEVIN,'" JOURNEY

CHAPTER SEVEN

THE GOALS

"My Maserati does 185."

"LIFE'S BEEN GOOD," JOE WALSH

NOW THAT YOU HAVE A BIG-PICTURE DREAM etched in your mind, you can begin to set specific goals for living your dream. Let me let you in on a little secret when it comes to accomplishing the dreams we discussed in the last chapter. It comes from Mike Dooley's *Notes from the Universe*:

> *"Little tiny dreams require little tiny thoughts and little tiny steps.*
> *Great big dreams require great big thoughts and little tiny steps.*
> *Do I paint a clear picture?"*

THE UNIVERSE

Goals are good because they can be broken down into smaller steps. Goals provide focus and clarity and paint the target that your mind aims for consciously and subconsciously. When your mind is fixed on a goal, creativity soars as your brain searches for a way to accomplish the goal that has been set. Your mind also begins to align itself with the natural flow of the Universe, and the law of attraction then begins to bring you the material and energy sources that are needed to realize the goal at hand. Without a goal, you are likely to drift aimlessly through the Universe like a rudderless and unmanned boat in the great big ocean of life. How can you hit a bull's-eye if you don't have a target to shoot at?

Setting and achieving goals are like anything else—you need to immerse yourself in the practice of goal setting so you can master the art of setting and accomplishing goals. However, before we launch into the actual mechanics of setting goals, let's take a page out of the playbook of executive coach and host of the *Get-It-Done Guy* podcast Steven Robbins. Robbins advocates for setting goals that define the journey as much as the outcome.[8] Much like Mike Dooley, he suggests you answer the following questions to choose a "life direction" rather than "life goals":

- How do I want to spend my time?

- What daily activities make me want to leap out of bed?

- What do I want to learn?

- Who do I want to hang out with? Talk with? Collaborate with?

This makes perfect sense to me. As you will soon see, the best things in life are the things you get from engaging in what motivational speakers refer to as "inspired action." Getting my son out of bed in the morning during his middle school days ranged something between a challenge and an all-out war. However, when I took him on a private guided salmon tour while on vacation in Alaska, he had no problem leaping out of bed at 3:00 a.m. Funny how that works. If you can find a line of work that you enjoy so much that it does not usually feel like work, then you are on the right path. If it turns out that the path you follow not only keeps you happy and fulfilled in the moment but also can bring to you the "thing" goals in life, then you are really rocking your life.

In short, this is a book about making decisions that make sense but also feel right. Pick something that can get you to your destination, develops you as a person, and at the end of the day makes you happy. If you associate too much pain with reaching for your goal, chances are you will quit.

Are there exceptions? Yes. There are some pursuits that are thoroughly engaging but are unlikely to produce enough income in the present to create the life you imagine. A perfect example of this is one of my adjunct law professors. Earlier in his career he left the practice of law to move to Los Angeles and pursue his true passion of being a jazz pianist. After a couple of years of trying to make it full time in the music business, he found that he could make more money, predictably, practicing law than he could as a full-time musician. Hence, he returned to the practice of law and is now one of the leading legal authorities on his niche practice area. And guess what he does for fun? He still performs gigs as a jazz pianist. His law practice provides the opportunity to support his passion for music, and his passion for music drives him to master his area of law. Consequently, he excels at both.

For many of us, it does not make immediate sense to simply quit a day job and become a full-time songwriter. However, if you begin to spend just fifteen minutes a day on writing songs, learn the craft of songwriting, and research how to get published, you will be surprised by the momentum you can create. This is exactly what I did, and through my faith and my focus, I wound up collaborating with a Grammy Award-winning songwriter even though I do not play any instruments and can't sing. My zeal for songwriting also brought new meaning and purpose to my work because it was supporting my songwriting efforts.

Decide how important money is to you. As I've mentioned, there is nothing wrong with being motivated by and possessing money. Why do you value money? Most of us, I suspect, associate money with words like *freedom, security, peace of mind, status, power,* and *leisure.* Having money allows you to enjoy the things in life that you like to have or like to do. Personally, when I focus on making money for its own sake, I don't feel inspired. However, when I know what I am playing for and when I am engaging in activities that make me feel good while being paid, it is easier for me to attract money into my life.

If I simply think about "the practice of law," I don't feel inspired. In fact, I associate a sense of uneasiness and stress with the thought of "practicing law," which is a demanding and pressure-filled profession. However, when I think about my estate planning practice, where I am mentally engaged and where I get to become intimately involved in discussing my clients' backgrounds, family dynamics, and helping them to plan their legacies, I feel inspired and energized. After a client meeting where these matters are discussed, I often think that I can't believe I get paid for doing something I love. Love what you do, do it well, and the money will come. Money is indeed important to me, but the way I go about earning it is important to me too.

"Yes, there are two paths you can go by,
but in the long run
there's still time to change
the road you're on."
"STAIRWAY TO HEAVEN," LED ZEPPELIN

Over the years I have studied and implemented many different goal-setting methods. The important thing is to have a structure in place that allows you to set your goals, commit your goals to writing, and then take action (little steps) to move toward that goal. Following are two separate approaches to goal achievement for your consideration. The first approach is a ninety-day goal-setting method that will narrow your focus and jump-start you toward success. It will also begin to condition your mind to know that the goal you are setting is real and that it must, it can, and it is being reached. The second method is the popular "SMART" goal method that can be applied to anything you want to be, do, or have.

NINETY-DAY GOAL SETTING

To bring goals to life—and establish an achievement mind-set—it is useful to start by setting ninety-day goals. Ninety-day goals are especially powerful if you are just beginning to set goals for yourself or if you have struggled with reaching longer-term goals. The more accomplished goal setter can also find value in setting ninety-day goals since a short time frame helps crystalize one's true priorities in the coming three months. Although I have often set ninety-day goals, the particular method I am about to describe was first brought to my attention by Jonathan Milligan, founder of Blogging Your Passion.

The beauty of the ninety-day goal time frame is that it narrows your focus on just a few very specific goals, or outcomes. Second, it incorporates specific "performance goals" into your ninety-day game plan that will carry you to your desired outcome. Third, by narrowing your focus to a few specific objectives, ninety-day goals instill an inherent inner faith that you can really get the job done. Then, as you actually achieve your ninety-day goals, you can take on bigger and longer-term goals armed with the knowledge that you have successfully achieved goals you have set for yourself. Here, then, is Milligan's Five Step process for setting—and achieving—your ninety-day goals.

STEP ONE: Choose Less Than Five Outcome Goals

This step is broken down into parts A, B, and C as follows:

- *PART A: Set your outcome goals*—Personally, I think one to three goals is all that you should choose. Life always comes down to priorities, and I want you to create laser-like focus. I want you to strengthen the goal-achievement aspect of your life so that you can begin to go after your big dream with more strength, faith, and courage. By achieving your ninety-day goals, you will gain confidence by knowing that you have the power to actually achieve the goals you establish for yourself. In time, you will come to understand that goal achievement is not so much about what you *get* but rather what you *become* during the process. Goal achievement results in the development of some of the best self-esteem you will ever build for yourself! After completing a draft of my book, my ninety-day goal was to finish and publish this book! Notice how this one goal supports my "Big Dream" to be a published author.

- *PART B: Set a few performance goals for each outcome goal*—Here we want to use goals that are "measurable." For me, I set a goal to edit one chapter per week. For example, this week, I will complete the rewrite of my chapter entitled "The Goals." To do this, I committed to spend at least the first thirty minutes of my workday editing my book. This was an easy thing to measure for either I have spent a half hour working on my book or I have not. By committing to this specific time frame, I was also able to monitor my progress to determine whether thirty minutes a day was sufficient to edit one chapter per week. Notice that by devoting the first thirty minutes of the work-day to writing my book, I am focusing my attention on making my dreams and myself a priority. This is a simple, yet powerful, demonstration of self-love.

- *PART C: Establish your process goals*—This is where Milligan states that "your performance goal won't happen until you establish the when, where, and what." What time of the day will you work on your goal? Where will you be? What will you do? For me, it was upon arrival to the office that I would close my door and devote the first thirty minutes of my work-day to editing this book. Although that sounds easy, it forced me to really work on planning my day in advance (see chapter 8) and sometimes delegating, deleting, or deferring other "to-do items." If I missed a day, I would have to figure out how to make it up either later that day or the next day or on a weekend. Sometimes, I would have to arrive ridiculously early at my office, like 4:00 a.m., before heading off to a court appearance.

STEP TWO: Write Your Goals in a Visible Location

Whether you use sticky notes, a whiteboard, index cards, or something else, write down your goals and keep them in front of your nose. Remember this creed: "It is not a goal unless it is written down." Tape your writ-ten goals to the ceiling above your bed so you can see them first thing in the morning and last thing at night.

Don't skip this step because a written goal is often the very first outer manifestation of your light, voice, and vision. In fact, read your goals out loud in the morning and at night before going to bed. If you have voice-memo capability, then, at a minimum, record yourself reading your goals and listen to the recording in the morning and at night.

STEP THREE: Turn Your Goals into One- to Two-Week Performance Goals

When I train for a marathon, I have a very specific sixteen-week plan that is broken down by the week. Each week builds upon the prior week. Sunday is my slow-recovery run after a long run on Saturday. Monday is an off day. Tuesday is either a speed day or what is known as "lactate threshold" running day. My Wednesday and Thursday runs are at slower, more comfortable paces. Friday is an off day, and Saturday may begin with an eight-mile run at the inception of the training regimen, and as the weeks progress, I build to twenty miles. The idea is that each run has its own specific objective and each training session is interrelated. Over time, my running improves, and I become stronger rather than wearing myself down physically and mentally.

STEP FOUR: Crush Procrastination with the Who, When, Where, and What Principle

Refer back to part C of step one. This is where the rubber meets the road and where you will see your daily actions begin to pay off. Stick to the plan. Stay true to yourself. Even if it is a difficult or unpleasant task, attack it. You will always feel relieved or better afterward. When I have a doctor's appointment, I keep it no matter what else is going on. Have that same level of commitment when you schedule an appointment with yourself. Don't make excuses for yourself or play the part of a victim of circumstance. As Zig Ziglar was fond of saying, "When you are tough on yourself, life is going to be infinitely easier on you."

STEP FIVE: Start Each Day with a Focus Session to Crush Your Goals

It's amazing how, if you spend the beginning of each day—whether you begin with fifteen minutes or two hours a day—doing what you love and/or working on self-development to become stronger physically, mentally, emotionally, and spiritually, over time this can become your daily existence.

Another critical step is taking time, at least once a week, to track your progress. The idea here is to view this as a reward session so that your brain links pleasure to reviewing your progress. For example, you may wish to schedule time each week to sit down with a coffee at Starbucks while reviewing your goals. Regardless of when or where you do it, you must take the time to evaluate whether or not:

- You are actually doing what you say you set out to do.

- You are diligent with your effort.

- Your efforts are working.

If the above statements are not true, identify the obstacles you must overcome and what resources are needed to overcome them. Don't waste valuable time by getting off course. Splashing a lot of water around may keep you busy, but unless you are actually swimming toward your destination, you are not being effective.

SMART GOALS

One of the most common goal-setting methods (because it works) is referred to by its acronym "SMART" goals. Let's take a look:

S = Specific

"I want to be rich" is not specific. "I want to have in my possession $1 million within the next five years" is specific. Choose a *specific* goal because then you can have a specific target to aim for. (Think *bull's-eye*). Take five minutes right now and write down three specific goals: One "thing" goal, one "do" goal, and one "be" goal. For example: *I want a Maserati that does 185, I want to run a marathon, I want to be a published author.*

M = Measurable

Again, referring to the examples above, you either obtain a $1 million or you don't. There is no way of knowing whether you reach a nonspecific goal of "I want to be rich."

A = Achievable

This book is premised on faith and infinite possibilities, so aim high. However, it also preaches the voice of reason, so pick something that is achievable—then you can go higher. If you choose something so massive that your brain can't fathom it, it will be difficult for you to stay on track to achieve the goal. One great way of achieving a "reach for the stars" goal is to break it down. For example, if you want to make a $1 million within the next five years, you will want to break it down to yearly goals. It might then look something like this:

Year 1	Year 2	Year 3	Year 4	Year 5
$300,000	$450,000	$600,000	$800,000	$1,000,000

R = Realistic

By all means, dream big! There is, after all, a theory that says, "Shoot for the moon, for even if you miss, you will land among the stars." However, when you break down your goals, you want to choose a target that may be difficult but still within your realm. Qualifying for and running the Boston Marathon was a difficult but realistic goal for me to shoot for, and I am proud to say I did both. However, if my goal was to win the Boston Marathon, I would have been setting myself up for certain failure (unless, of course, I wanted to attempt what Rosie Ruiz did in 1980 when she jumped on the Boston Marathon course around mile 25 and ran the last mile ahead of the first woman competitor)!

T = Time (Deadline)

There is nothing like a deadline to make something happen. Deadlines have a way of creating a sense of urgency and certainty in pursuit of one's goals. Without a deadline, you will never actually have to hold yourself accountable for fulfilling a goal, and you will never feel pressed to do so. How you invest your time, talents, and treasure boils down to a value choice. As I've already mentioned, my suspicion is that most of us are lazy by nature, and it is only when we have a strong enough reason to act that we spring into action. A deadline forces you to focus on how you will devote your energy at any given time. A deadline also stimulates creativity because when something has to get done immediately, your brain will search for an answer—and there is always an answer.

Now that we are ready to set SMART goals, we can choose our specific goals. Warning: your dream life is drawing near, and there is no turning back now!

CHOOSING GOALS

Now that you have a SMART mentality, you can establish three types of goals: "Financial goals," "thing goals," and "be and do goals."

Financial Goals

Financial goals can be set in the form of a specific amount of money, for example, "I want my personal net worth to be $1 million within the next five years." You can also state them as income goals, for example,

"I want to make $300,000 in income this year." Take a few minutes now to write down your financial goals for one, three, and five years. Make sure they are SMART goals. Then, for each goal, write down three actions you can take toward the achievement of this goal. Place a deadline after each activity. Then schedule a specific time when you will complete the goal. If you can take one immediate action right now, so much the better. The point is to gain forward momentum so that you can then track your progress.

One Year:_____

    1._____

    2._____

    3._____

Three Years: _____

    1._____

    2._____

    3._____

Five Years:_____

    1._____

    2._____

    3._____

Thing Goals

There is nothing wrong with having things. The preceding chapters have professed that we all come from one energy source and one substance, the God Particle, and we have every entitlement to material things as much as anyone else in the world does. Dare to dream for the things in life that you really desire! Do you want a Mercedes? Oceanfront property? A wine collection?

Pick three things for each of the three time periods shown below and resolve to have each item by the chosen time frame. One cautionary note is that scientists have confirmed that having material possessions is not as meaningful as "doing things." Still, it's nice to indulge and live in opulence! Surrounding yourself with material pleasures helps create a proper state of mind that allows you to move more harmoniously toward your goals. Once again, schedule a specific time on your calendar to undertake three activities for each possession. It may be as simple as looking up the name of a car dealership.

One Year:_____

   1._____

   2._____

   3._____

Three Years: _____

   1._____

2. _____

3. _____

Five Years: _____

1. _____

2. _____

3. _____

Be and Do Goals

I have saved the best for last (again, as borne out by scientific research). Where do you wish to travel? What do you wish to create? Music? Artwork? A book? Do you want to learn how to dance? Cook? Whatever is lurking within you is about to unfold because, once you place it in writing, you have begun your journey.

Again, these are things you want to spend your time working on. These are the things that will bring you happiness and an inner sense of fulfillment. For me, being a single-digit handicap golfer is important because, by achieving that one goal, so many of my other goals in terms of time for leisure, material possessions, and financial prosperity will also have been met. Prioritize the things you want most, but still make sure the goals are SMART goals. Note, I do not place a limit here in terms of how many things you want to do or achieve because you may have one overriding goal that trumps all others. For example, if you want to be a professional golfer, then most of your time will be devoted to playing and practicing golf. Again, schedule time to work on your goals. Pretty soon your dreams will begin to come true!

CONDENSE YOUR GOALS

Now that you have your goals in order, you will want to write them down in such a way as to be able to review them each morning, day, and night. Perhaps you can place them on an index card and keep the card in your wallet for easy reference. Or you can create a vision board of all the things you want. Get excited, have fun, and be grateful that you have the ability to pull off your goals. This is the time, and you are about to have the time of your life! In the next chapter, we will delve deeper into the actual planning that you will undertake to meet these goals you have just set for yourself.

FINAL THOUGHTS ON GOAL SETTING

Setting and reaching for a goal is really just a test of how committed you are to achieving it. You must make certain in your mind that you are committed to achieving the goal you set. Write down why each goal is important to you. If you have a compelling reason to reach a destination, the chances increase exponentially that you will get there. The human spirit can overcome virtually any obstacle and, under certain circumstances, risk everything to obtain a desired outcome. You must have faith that you can—and a paramount reason to be successful.

How else can you explain a mom jumping in front of

an SUV rolling toward a cliff to save her three children? How else could a middle-aged grandmother lift a full-sized car off her grandson who was pinned beneath it? Why is it that the person who survives a heart attack suddenly makes diet and exercise a top priority? Spend the time thinking about which goals really matter to you and why. Then go after those goals with full vigor until they become your reality. One caveat though: if your goals no longer make sense for you, set new ones that do. Don't be a slave to accomplishment for accomplishment's sake alone. Such misplaced energy often leads to stress, disease, and unhappiness. Goals are meant to be uplifting and not intended to be your master!

EXERCISE

➤ Answer Stever Robbins's questions on page 86.

➤ Do not continue reading until you have committed your goals to writing and condensed your goals.

➤ Spend time answering why any particular goal is so vital to your well-being.

➤ Choose one to three goals you are committed to achieving in the next ninety days and put them in writing. Then, take the time to follow the five steps starting on page 90. Alternatively, set in writing "financial" goals, "thing" goals, and "be" goals following the SMART goal method outlined in this chapter.

- Answer these questions: What time of the day will you work on your goal? Where will you be? What will you do?

- Keep your goals in front of you and refer to them often.

- Schedule a time with yourself at least weekly to measure your progress. What do you need to do more of or less of to achieve your goals?

- Follow your light, visualize yourself achieving your goal, and keep your voice focused on "I must, I can, and I am" reaching my goals.

- Don't stop believing, and don't quit until you reach your goals.

- Remember to be tough on yourself so that life will be infinitely easier on you.

- Enjoy the journey!

"I've made my mind up that it's meant to be, Someday lady you'll accomp'ny me."

"YOU'LL ACCOMPANY ME," BOB SEGAR

CHAPTER EIGHT

THE PLAN

"Take a look ahead."

"PEACE OF MIND," *BOSTON*

A FEW YEARS BACK, I WAS WATCHING my thirteen-year-old daughter Megan's travel soccer game and observing the girls playing with great passion and desire. It was, after all, a tournament championship game, and it just so happened that her team was playing their crosstown rivals. Both teams played their heart out with equal force, intensity, and desire (read: *passion*). Hence, passion alone would not have been enough on its own to carry the day, for each team played with great passion. Instead, the outcome of the game was the result of a well-executed and planned-out play by Megan's team that led to the winning goal. This, to me, is a simple example of how having passion (in this case, for the game of soccer) can be integrated with reason (in this case, proper execution of a designed play) to obtain a desired outcome.

However, I observed something else about this

game. When Megan first started playing soccer at the age of five, both teams followed the ball the way a swarm of bees follow a queen bee. At that age, children are not (and should not be) taught the strategic implications of spreading the players out across the field to better help the team. They also are not taught to keep their head up when they possess the ball and to look to pass the ball to a teammate or to shoot at the goal before they dribble into pressure.

By age thirteen, however, the players have been schooled over and over again about the basic tenets of spreading out across the field rather than blindly swarming to the ball. They have also been instructed, when in possession of the ball, to pass the ball before it's too late. To be sure, at age thirteen, you can see glimpses of the girls doing just that. Players spreading out across the field looks far better than it did in their younger years, but it's not perfect. Likewise, while there are some players, on some plays, who do get rid of the ball in advance of defenders taking away their options, the vast majority of plays end when a player will dribble until she is closed off by a defender and either loses the ball, makes a weak pass, or occasionally dribbles out of it. By not anticipating the pressure soon enough, the player who was open is no longer open. The open field is now cluttered with opposing players. The situation has changed for the worse.

As adults, we tend to be no different from children playing soccer or any other sport for that matter. Many of us simply do not anticipate what is coming in advance of the situation, and therefore, we do not make the proper adjustment until it's too late. This forces us into a reactive mode instead of a proactive state, and the options available are then usually more limited. Using an analogy from Tony Robbins, if you know that the rowboat is heading downstream toward Niagara Falls, doesn't it make sense to steer toward the shore well away from the falls rather than waiting until you are just a few feet away from disaster? Of course, it does.

Then why don't we do it? Why do we procrastinate? I have some thoughts. First, we procrastinate because we are lazy. Second, we allow the fear of uncertainty to stifle our progress. Third, we don't have enough facts, so we can't intelligently anticipate what is coming next. Fourth, we don't visualize in advance what we want. What, then, can we do about it? Before embarking upon a project of major importance, spend time thinking before you act. As my Jesuit priests in high school instructed, "Make haste slowly." Remember that organized thought is one of the most difficult undertakings for man to engage himself in.

Here are some steps to begin planning. First, go into the silence and spend five minutes or more in isolated thought, thinking through a situation. Second, form a mastermind group. In *Think and Grow Rich*, Napoleon Hill put this toward the top of his list for the achievement of riches. In essence, two or more minds can come up with better plans and ideas than a single mind can. Thus, do not go it alone. Third, determine if there is critical information missing, and if so, figure out how you can obtain more information. Knowledge is power as long, of course, as the power is harnessed and used effectively. Finally, once a project has begun, you simply must take time to analyze the results of actions already taken and determine what is and isn't working and why. Can you imagine if NASA did not plan obsessively for sending a man to the moon?

If you are about to embark upon a project of major importance to you, do not simply wing it. Heed the words of Napoleon Hill, who said that one must have flawless plans if he is to obtain riches.

Proper planning strikes at the heart of the law of attraction. Players or people who wait until it's too late or nearly too late are attracting trouble into their lives that could have been avoided in the first place. Albert Einstein said, "A clever person solves a problem. A wise person avoids it." Moreover, advanced planning increases the odds that one can more readily control the outcome of situation upon their own terms. For example, airplane pilots have extensive checklists that must be used before every flight. By going through those checklists, the odds of a safe flight are greatly increased.

However, even in the event that something goes wrong during a flight, pilots are trained to deal with the emergency. By having a predetermined response to an emergency situation, pilots once again are in a much stronger position to determine the outcome than had no such planning took place. This is yet another example where great passion and desire will need to be channeled intelligently by entertaining quality, pro-active thoughts to get from where you are to where you want to go. In other words, "Take a look ahead!"

Benjamin Franklin said, "For every minute spent in organizing, an hour is earned." If you are going to advance confidently in the direction of your dreams and achieve the goals you set for yourself in the last chapter, chances are you will have to get organized. Organization is just another way of saying that you will need to establish your priorities. Unless you take control of setting your own priorities and organize your activities around your priorities, you will have to accept the priorities that others set for you and your use of time, treasure, and talents.

This is why having a big-picture dream and then measurable achievable goals is so important. By breaking each goal down into single identifiable steps, it is much easier to stay on track and avoid a feeling of being overwhelmed. Of course, part of the planning process includes establishing your priorities and developing strategies that will allow you to manifest your dreams and visions. Returning then to the goals that you set for yourself, let's further narrow our focus and develop the actual strategies, techniques, and activities that will be employed to accomplish your goals.

FINANCIAL GOALS

There are only three ways to increase your income if you are selling products or services: you either must sell more units or services, you must increase the price of your goods or services, or you must cut expenses. As your income grows, more opportunities will open up for you that will cause a paradigm shift for you—the better you become at sales, the more better opportunities will come to you—remember Jim Rohn's quote on the law of attraction: "Success is not something you pursue. What you pursue will elude you. It can be like trying to chase butterflies. Success is something you attract and accumulate by the person you become."

A typical sales funnel will look for prospects that lead to sales calls that lead to proposals that lead to closing deals that lead to "up selling" additional products or services. If you become good at the process and execute it faithfully, you will inevitably become a successful person and attract success. If you are in sales, spend a few minutes now and determine what you must do to fill your funnel with prospects and then commit to setting a standard you will live up to on a quarterly, monthly, weekly, daily, and, in some cases, even an hourly basis.

If you have been averaging two sales appointments a week, figure out what it will take to get a third one, and you can then measure your success and predict the increased income. Again, you have faith, and by focusing now on the activities that will determine success, you will inevitably attract more success by being an attractive person.

If you are not in a sales position, then you will have to figure out how you will get a new job or career path that will give you the increased income. If you want a new career but lack education or current skills, then begin at once to start to acquire whatever it is you need to move forward. Start with something easy—maybe google the local university to see what evening classes or programs are available to you.

If you are not working for a living but wish to increase your income, begin developing a plan that will bring more money into your life. It may be a business idea, an investment strategy, or some other endeavor.

THING GOALS

Is a new Mercedes in your future? Then by all means begin to visualize it and cut a picture out to put on your vision board. Go to a dealership and test-drive it. I am all for it. However, don't stop there. Continue to ask yourself (inner voice), "What else can I do to bring me closer to my Mercedes?" Find out how much it will cost to finance. If you have credit issues, start now to clean up your credit. Review your budget and see what current expenses you may be able to reduce or other things you can do without, and you will begin to see how you can make the monthly payment.

DO GOALS

When I decided to write this book, I made it easy on myself. My goal was to spend the first fifteen minutes of my workday writing this book. By mostly sticking to this schedule, two things happened. First, pages began to fill up. Second, I gained momentum and my fifteen minutes turned into longer periods. It was not written in a day. Third, new ideas came to light because I was constantly focusing on writing the book—in other words, it was a reality to me that this book would be written. This is the difference between merely possessing blind faith in a desired outcome versus having a dream backed by faith with focus.

RELATIONSHIP GOALS

If you are looking to attract that special someone in your life and the bar scene or dating sites aren't cutting it, then the answer is not to give up on your dream or goal; the answer is to change your focus, strategy, and plan. If it were me, I would start engaging in activities that I love to do, such as golfing, fishing, and traveling, and I would look for group activities to participate in. If the problem is shyness around the opposite sex, I would start really small. I might begin with a simple, authentic compliment to an attractive woman, e.g., "That is a beautiful dress that you have on tonight." The goal would not be to wind up with that woman; the goal would be to express attractiveness to a woman, and when you do it, you have succeeded. Then increase the number of compliments each day, and pretty soon, you will see what begins to happen. Conversely, if a woman gave me a compliment, I would smile and reply with an enthusiastic "Thank you!"

By engaging in activities you enjoy, you will inevitably become a happier and more cheerful person. In turn, you become more attractive. Others may soon introduce someone to you. Vince Lombardi said it best: "The will to win is not nearly so important as the will to prepare to win." Start planning, take action, and then act as if your goals are being met and pretty soon they will be!

THE SECRET FIRST STEP!

Success leaves clues—if you know where you want to go but don't know how to start putting things in action, find someone to model. One of the fastest ways to get from where you are now to where you want to go is to observe the people around you who are already living the type of life you want. That is, by modeling the behavior of successful people, you can fast-track your way to success. This concept, often referred to as modeling, is so critical that Tony Robbins labels it as one of the three steps toward achieving massive instant success.

For example, say you aspire to be the next Sir Richard Branson. You could begin to study his methods by reading his books, listening to his interviews, and paying attention to the people he conducts business with. In fact, once you focus your attention, you will be shocked by the circumstances, events, and people that will appear in your life that relate to Richard Branson.

At any rate, by learning as much as you can about Richard Branson's modus operandi, your intention has been set and unleashed into the Universe. Your job from here on is to go with the flow and set additional desires that relate to your end result. For example, an excellent intention to set would be to meet with Mr. Branson personally and do a business deal with him. Start by identifying one of his organizations and then contact someone in the organization to find out how to submit a business proposal to him. This will, of course, attract more business associations into your life.

Do not listen to your doubts. The secret to your success may begin with as little as one phone call. Or it may be a thousand calls away. Either way, as long as you are enjoying the journey in the direction of your end result, who cares how long it takes?

EXERCISE

➤ Pick out someone you admire, study their methods, and begin to model their behavior.

➤ Determine what you must do to master your chosen field of endeavor (or a hobby) and then set upon a course toward mastery.

➤ Review your goals from chapter 7 and, starting today, spend at least fifteen minutes a day developing a written plan for them, and then take at least one step that the plan calls for.

➤ Schedule a weekly appointment with yourself to review your progress and plan your next week's activities. Do not skip this step. Treat your appointment with yourself as if it were an important doctor's appointment that you will not cancel.

➤ Find at least one other person you can mastermind with on a regular basis.

➤ Start planning for your success and happiness.

➤ Take a look ahead!

*"I can see clearly now the rain is gone
I can see all obstacles in my way."*

"I CAN SEE CLEARLY NOW," JOHNNY NASH

CHAPTER NINE

THE TIME

"Does anybody really know what time it is?
Does anybody really care (about time)?"

"DOES ANYBODY REALLY KNOW
WHAT TIME IT IS," CHICAGO

EINSTEIN HAD A THEORY THAT THE PAST, the present, and the future all exist simultaneously. Time, in Einstein's view, has to do with the speed of light. The faster you can keep up with the speed of light, the less the fabric of time is encompassed. In Einstein's mind, this explained why time is relative and not linear or absolute. Indeed, studies have proved Einstein's theory to be correct. To be sure, many modern-day scholars, physicists, quantum physicists, theorists, and inspirational leaders subscribe to Einstein's theory of simultaneous existence. As profound and interesting as Einstein's theory may be, it sure feels like there is such a thing as time when I face a fast-approaching deadline. It sure feels like I never have enough time when I am overwhelmed with more projects screaming for my attention than I can handle at once. It sure feels like there is something called time when I am stuck at a traffic light while running late for an appointment.

In fact, for me, the lack of time is a greater psychological barrier to achieving my goals than the lack of money. For me, the feeling of not having enough time to do the things I want to do is perhaps the single biggest limiting belief I have had to overcome. In this chapter, I wish to relate to you a new way of thinking about time, which can have a dramatic shift in your ability to master this seemingly fleeting resource. (Sorry, Einstein.) I will also provide you with practical tips that will have you focusing on your priorities and not time wasters.

Let's start with the truth—at least as we measure it. Each of us has 24 hours a day, which equals 86,400 seconds a day. Everyone, including the world's most successful people, have the same amount of time per day as the rest of us. In fact, the time between point A and point B is a great equalizer. Therefore, we are not being fair to ourselves or others when we say, "We don't have enough time." Having enough time is simply a matter of making a wise choice as to where we direct our energy and focus at any point in existence. (Maybe this is what Einstein was getting at.) From this moment forward, never allow yourself to finish the sentence "I don't have enough time." Catch yourself instead and resolve that "I have more than enough time, and I choose how to use it." This simple recalibration will shift your focus from being a victim of time to being a self-directed investor of time. It's within your own personal power to use time in the way that you want to invest it.

If time is really a focus issue, then the next question is how do we determine what to focus on?

What Are Your Priorities?

"The key is not to prioritize what's on your schedule, but rather to schedule your priorities."
STEVEN COVEY

At any given moment, our attention may be directed to several different things. To maintain a road map to stay on track toward accomplishing your goals, it is important to determine in advance what your priorities are. When these priorities are crystal clear in your mind, then it is easier to determine where you should be investing your time when more than one choice presents itself.

For example, if your top priority is to launch a new business, then most of your choices on how to invest your time will be geared toward activities that support getting your business off the ground. However, while it may appear simple to select that activity among competing choices that results in the highest and best use of your time, you may unwittingly be yielding to competing forces, both internally and externally, that can redirect your focus toward other behaviors. Let's briefly examine the forces that often dictate how you *actually* spend your time versus how you *planned* to spend your time.

Our Thoughts

Our thoughts determine how we spend our time. Since we predominantly think about the same things the vast amount of time, we spend most of our time each day doing (or not doing) the same things. If you are feeling overwhelmed, it is because you are overloading your choices of activities and not breaking things down to manageable activities. Start breaking down your duties into specific finite tasks and then go about completing each task in order of importance.

Our Feelings

The way we feel at any given moment drives our behavior. When we feel unstoppable, we go for it; when we like what we are doing, we go for it; when we fear doing something, we tend to hesitate or altogether avoid the activity we fear. Notice how your feelings affect the behaviors you *actually* engage in versus the behaviors you *intend* to engage in. Also, pay attention to how your feelings affect the amount of intensity you are putting into your actions. There are times when you simply must stay on task even if you don't particularly feel like it. Keep the end result in mind.

Other People

Jim Rohn had a great quote about the impact other people have on your time: "If you don't design your own life plan, chances are you'll fall into someone else's plan. And guess what they have planned for you? Not much." If you really wish to master your time, begin by choosing for yourself how you will invest your time and not let others dictate your schedule. Again, this becomes easier when you know what your top priorities are.

Values

We talk about "time," and we talk about "values," but rarely do we link the two. If you are having trouble figuring out what your value system is, I suggest you start by keeping a time log. Mark down each activity for a couple of days, and record how much time you spend doing each thing. Soon a pattern will emerge. For example, if you have a great career but are struggling on the family front, then you may be devoting more time to your career at the expense of your family. If you pride yourself as a "family first " person but spend little time with the family, then maybe you need to reexamine what your priorities are. It also works the other way around. You may be spending so much family time that your business is suffering. Balancing priorities may be difficult, but you must begin to figure out where you are investing your time, energy, and focus before you can begin to figure out a way to pursue your dreams.

INTERRUPTIONS

What is an interruption? The Merriam-Webster dictionary defines the word "interrupt" as "to cause or make a break in the continuity or uniformity of (a course, process, condition, etc.)."

Why are we easily interrupted? The easiest way to think of an interruption is anything that distracts your focus on what matters most to you. What are the recurring interruptions and distractions in your life? Do you have coworkers who regularly interrupt your train of thought with idle chatter? Is there a friend or family member who continually persuades you to do what he or she wants you to do instead of what you want to do? Do you fall prey to surfing the internet when you should be working on a project instead? Figure out what you must do to prevent or minimize those interruptions from happening in the future. It may be that you say yes to every request that someone makes of you because you want to be known as a nice person. Limit the areas of how you help people, and the more you can align your desire to help others with your career the better off everyone will be.

THE GREATEST USE OF TIME?

You eat to nourish your body. You sleep to rejuvenate your spirit. You study, work, and apply yourself for emotional gains. You exercise to tighten your muscles. You listen to music to entertain yourself.

You're not at all adverse to investing time and energy for the rewards you seek. So how about you spare just a few minutes every day to visualize the life of your dreams? Because nothing else you could ever do will make such a profound difference in your fortunes and misfortunes as working with your thoughts and beliefs.

You can start now,
The Universe[9]

SAYING NO

If you are serious about "saving time," you must learn the art of saying "no" politely. This is a tough chore for most us, and yet it can be one of the more liberating ideas in your life. Most of us associate significant pain with saying "no," so we find ourselves committing our time and energy to the whims of others. However, economists teach us that there is an "opportunity cost" to every activity we choose. Investopedia describes "opportunity cost" this way:

> Opportunity costs represent the benefits an individual, investor, or business *misses out on* when choosing one alternative over another. While financial reports do not show opportunity cost, business owners can use it to make educated decisions when they have multiple options before them. Because they are unseen by definition, opportunity costs can be overlooked if one is not careful. By understanding the potential missed opportunities one forgoes by choosing one investment over another, better decisions can be made.[10]

As it relates to time management, choosing one activity comes at the expense of foregoing engaging in another activity. Great "time managers" tend to have a natural ability to calculate the "opportunity cost" before deciding which path to take. Begin at once to focus on the opportunity cost of doing or not doing something and watch as your time becomes better invested in the areas of life that matter most to you.

RULE OF FIVE

The marketing formula that I selected to market *Faith With Focus* is the "rule of five" as that concept is articulated in Jack Canfield's book *The Success Principles*. The rule-of-five approach works well with a large and time-consuming project. As Canfield explains:

> I suggest making a list each day of five action steps that will move you closer to your goal. Then check them off as you complete each one. Be very specific in your actions. If your breakthrough goal is to achieve your ideal weight, one day might look like this:
>
> **My five action steps today:**
> 1. Do morning stretches for 10 minutes.
> 2. Walk for 30 minutes.
> 3. Prepare a healthy lunch with plenty of green vegetables.
> 4. Go grocery shopping right after lunch so that I don't shop when I am hungry.
> 5. Spend 15 minutes visualizing how I will look and feel when I achieve my goal or reading my affirmations.
>
> The cumulative effect of these daily steps can be profound. Small action steps are manageable, and achieving them daily keeps you motivated and your momentum strong. Whether your goal is to drop 20 pounds, run a marathon, start a business, or *write a book,* apply the Rule of Five each day and see what "miracles" you create in your life. [Italics supplied][11]

I love the rule-of-five concept because it is a shining example of how focus can strengthen your faith and faith strengthens focus. It is also a strategy that is easy to plan and easy to execute. For me, I developed a list of twenty promotional activities to market my book, and I simply go down the menu of items and select which five I will work on that day (or sometimes that week). Regardless of your dream or the goals you have set for yourself, start at once to implement the rule of five and see magic and miracles appear in your life!

SET IT AND FORGET IT!

I remember watching the Ron Popeil infomercials where he sold the Ronco Rotisserie, the number-one selling rotisserie in the world. His famous tag line was "Set it and forget it." His message was clear: by buying his rotisserie (which I did), you could easily make delicious chicken. "Set it and forget it" saved time in the kitchen! Apply a "set it and forget it" method whenever you can in your life. When there is an opportunity to automate a function or implement a repeatable process in your routine, make the decision to invest the time up front to establish the automated system that will save you untold hours in the future. "Set it and forget it" applies to all areas of your life, including finances, and can actually improve your performance. A June 2015 article[12] in *Forbes* magazine said this:

> New Year's Day exists for an important reason. It's the day many investors make a resolution to save more and invest better. But then June rolls around

and we find that it hasn't happened. By summer, there's less money for savings and investment skills have not improved. That's why a year-round, "Set It and Forget It" investment strategy using low-cost index funds should be part of your next New Year's resolve. Automation is the key to a successful savings and investing plan.

By "automation," I'm saying a strategy needs to happen automatically, before your biased brain has time to get in the way of your best habits.

Automate as much as you can and the sands of time will begin to tip in your favor!

PROCRASTINATE LATER

Instinctively, we know that when we focus our attention on meaningful activities that support our light, vision, goals, dreams, and purpose, we are far less likely to procrastinate. That is an inherent theme of *Faith With Focus*. In the next chapter on inspired action, we will see how time flies when we engage in activities that inspire us. Additionally, when our actions are aligned with our values, we tend to move effortlessly through our days. Nonetheless, we would be hard-pressed to find an individual who never procrastinates. Nearly everyone has difficulty facing an unpleasant task or situation that needs to be addressed. We are all guilty of procrastination from time to time.

Since it often does not make sense to quit the day job while transitioning to a new line of work, you may be stuck doing tasks that you don't feel like doing and resolving issues that you don't feel like confronting.

Know, however, that when you responsibly accept the task at hand and perform it admirably, or when you meet an unpleasant issue head-on, you are moving in the general direction of your dream. You are building self-confidence that you are willing to do what is necessary. Pat yourself on the back each time you complete such a task or confront such an issue, and soon enough these tasks won't be so unpleasant.

There are millions of articles that address ways in which to overcome procrastination. They boil down to first acknowledging that you procrastinate, determining why (fear, disorganization, unpleasant task), and then implementing strategies to overcome your procrastination. One buzz phrase that has helped me battle procrastination is "procrastinate later." When you procrastinate, you are not focusing on what you should be doing.

When I focus on what I know I should be doing and then do it–I always feel better about completing the task. That is my internal reward system. For example, earlier today I had to make a difficult phone call to turn down an opportunity with a person I think very highly of. It was a tough conversation. Rather than wait, I tackled it the first thing this morning and felt great afterward. I now have the freedom to totally immerse myself in my writing. I have also strengthened my self-esteem by having the grit to do the right thing and make that call. Remember the words of Zig Ziglar: "When you do the things you need to do when you need to do them, the day will come when you can do the things you want to do when you want to do them."

BE PROACTIVE

You are probably familiar with the old saying, "Hurry up and wait." In my experience, most people act in the exact opposite way: they wait and then hurry up. While this may be closely akin to procrastination, it also has to do with failure to focus on your destination and take the actions necessary to get there. The people who tend to get on in this world tend to be proactive. They master the art of getting things done correctly the first time around and in a timely fashion. Stay proactive in life. Remain alert about what needs to be done and by when, and then resolve to become good at getting your stuff done. You'd be surprised by how much more productive you can be and how much more time you will have to do the fun things in life.

TAKING LIFE AT YOUR OWN PACE

One of the biggest tragedies in human existence is that other people determine our deadlines and force us to live in accordance with their time parameters. Consequently, we don't get to take life at our own pace. I once took a psychological profile test that compared a person's temperament to three types of horses: the thoroughbred, the trotter, and the plough horse. Which best defines your pace?

For some reason, everyone expects us to be thoroughbreds, but not all of us are designed to move at that fast a pace. If your nature is more akin to a trotter horse, but you try to run like a thoroughbred or, worse, compete with them, the states of mind you are likely to encounter include anxiety, tension, neurosis, and feelings of self-defeat. Recall from chapter 1 that our light guides us. Do not feel the pressing need to get ahead of your light. Conversely, don't fall behind your light through mere laziness either. Let your light guide your pace. If everyone would just take life at their own pace and allow others to do the same, we would avoid many of the physical and mental ailments that plague industrial societies.

I have run eight marathons, and each time I chose my targeted pace. That decision was based on whether I was running the marathon with Mimi or whether I was out to set a personal record for myself (PR) such as in Chicago, where my goal was to set a PR and qualify for the Boston Marathon. (I did both with a time of 3:23:08.) That decision dictated my training schedule, my diet, my running partners, and my expectations. The same holds true for virtually everyone else in the marathon. Paces vary from world class times of two hours and five minutes to more than six hours, but everyone gets the same medal whether they finish first or last. Can you imagine if I was expected to compete with the winners? I would be beat down, defeated, and feeling bad.

Whatever your endeavor in life is, enjoy the process and take life at your own pace and you will find contentment. Don't fall prey to the dominate director who wants you to fulfill his or her dream by working for him or her at his or her pace. If you are a thoroughbred, then go for the gold. If you are a trotter, then move steadily toward your destination. If you are a plough horse, then move along at that pace (like the tortoise in the fable "The Tortoise and the Hare"), and you will find your own gold along the way.

EXERCISE

➢ As you go through your day today, pay attention to your thoughts and feelings and how they are impacting your decision on how to direct your energy and focus. Stop yourself from saying, "I don't have enough time" and interrupt it with "Time is on my side, yes, it is."

➢ Politely say no to someone else's demand for your time.

➢ Determine your priorities and schedule them on your calendar. Then stick to the schedule just the same as if you were keeping an important doctor's appointment.

➢ Pay attention to how you are spending time, wasting time, or investing time (keep a time log if possible).

➢ Start thinking about investing time rather than spending time.

➢ Schedule at least fifteen minutes to invest time in working on your plans and goals.

➢ Take life at your own pace (but keep moving)!

➢ Take the time to have the time of your life.

➢ Read the next chapter on inspired action, and time will never be your enemy again.

"Time, time, time is on my side, yes it is."
"TIME IS ON MY SIDE," THE ROLLING STONES

CHAPTER TEN

THE INSPIRED ACTION (AKA LOVE IN ACTION)

"Livin' on rock-n-roll music
Never worry 'bout the things we were missing
When we got up on stage
and got ready to play
Everybody'd listen."

"ROCK AND ROLL BAND," BOSTON

CAN YOU IMAGINE WHAT IT MUST BE LIKE to wake up every morning and "work" in a chosen career that does not feel like work at all? The answer by now should be *yes,* you can imagine it. The question then becomes "How can I get into a line of work that leaves me inspired and fulfilled at the end of the day rather than drained and frustrated?"

The answer begins by reviewing the last few chapters. We begin with a wild, crazy dream that we visualize in our mind. We act as if it has already come true, and our actions begin moving us in the direction of our dream. We follow our light, create our vision, and use our inner voice to set our direction and purpose in life. We feel the light in everything we do and let it radiate toward everyone we meet. We honor ourselves by loving ourselves and by treating ourselves well and others, too. Dream big! If your goal is to make $100,000 a year, then multiply it by ten.

When Tiger Woods was in his prime, I stated that if given the choice between having all his worldly possessions taken away from him or having his golf game taken away from him, he would choose the former. Little did I know then that Tiger Wood's world would soon crumble because he strayed from the core values he was raised with. At any rate, he has not regained the golf form he had before his troubles—at least not yet. However, you have not seen his desire to dominate fade despite injuries, swing changes, and naysayers. Tiger Woods, like all great champions, has hunger, and it is that hunger that fuels his activity. His never-ending quest to win again on the PGA tour became a reality when he won the 2018 tour championship, his first since 2013.

If you can find a line of work that meets your economic needs and provides you with the same kind of hunger that Tiger brings to the golf course, then you are living the life that the rock band Boston lived when they wrote, "Livin' on rock-and-roll music, never worry 'bout the things we were missing." This is the same burning desire that drove Henry Ford, Abraham Lincoln, Tiger Woods, Muhammad Ali, and all the rest of the great ones. Pick something that is suitable for you and something that you wish to master—to challenge yourself to master, not with the goal to outshine others around you–and you will be engaged in "inspired action."

The other way to unearth your hunger is to have a big enough reason to do something well. I remember a story a few years back about the mom and her child whose car got stuck in the middle of a western state like Wyoming in a bitter snowstorm. The mom was able to run 26 miles–the equivalent of a marathon–to bring her child to safety. The desire to protect her child was so powerful in her mind that it empowered her to reach well beyond her physical abilities and to overcome severe obstacles to save her child.

You do not have to wait to be put in a life-or-death situation to rescue your family. One simple example in my law practice is to educate parents on the importance of estate plans for the protection of their minor children. If something happens to the parents and there is no estate plan in place, the children can end up victims of an imperfect court system or an arbitrary family squabble. Their legal guardian may end up being someone other than who the parents would have chosen. Basic estate planning and life insurance can protect their children after the death or incapacitation of the parents.

Maybe you have started a business, and while it is starting to show signs of success, you are realizing it is a burden to sustain the business because you are shouldering all the responsibility and the daily requirements to keep the business afloat. The daily grind can take its toll on you mentally, physically, and spiritually. However, when you consider the bigger picture of the business financially supporting your family and providing a valuable service or product, it makes it easier to persevere through the tough times while you develop a better strategy that will allow you to enjoy even greater success and self-satisfaction again.

The point is you want to do something that is being fueled by your hunger and passion. When that happens for you, you are not just working but engaging in "inspired action."

Inspired action is just another way of expressing love. Love, as it turns out, is the central ingredient to all happiness. When I was in high school, I was asked to speak at a Christian retreat and the title of my presentation was "Love in Action." My talk was centered on the Bible verse: "So now faith, hope, and love abide, these three; but the greatest of these is love" (1 Corinthians 13:13, ESV). The sum and substance was that when we approach every situation and everyone with love (including our opponents), we are in a peak state. Conversely, when we treat others harshly or with disdain, we are in a negative state. Since positive emotions are infinitely stronger than negative ones, it pays to be in a state of love, which is the strongest positive emotion of all. What can make someone happier than being in love? Nothing! If you are having trouble in your marriage or with your children or a close family or friend, I suggest you start throwing love at the problem and see the love that you will attract back.

When you pour love into everything you do—especially the unpleasant tasks—you are letting your light shine. When you are talking to someone, be conscious of the love in your heart; when you are working, attack your job with love; when you are relaxing, exercising, or engaging in a recreational activity, feel the love that dwells within you.

The following excerpt is from an April 2013 post by Brent Lambert on Feelguide.com:

In 1938 Harvard University began following 268 male undergraduate students and kicked off the longest-running longitudinal studies of human development in history. The study's goal was to determine as best as possible what factors contribute most strongly to human flourishing. The astonishing range of psychological, anthropological, and physical traits—ranging from personality type to IQ to drinking habits to family relationships to "hanging length of his scrotum"—indicates just how exhaustive and quantifiable the research data has become. Recently, George Vaillant, who directed the study for more than three decades, published the study's findings in the 2012 book *Triumphs of Experience* (Amazon) and the following is the book's synopsis:

"At a time when many people around the world are living into their tenth decade, the longest longitudinal study of human development ever undertaken offers some welcome news for the new old age: our lives continue to evolve in our later years, and often become more fulfilling than before. Begun in 1938, the Grant Study of Adult Development charted the physical and emotional health of over 200 men, starting with their undergraduate days. The now-classic 'Adaptation to Life' reported on the men's lives up to age 55 and helped us understand adult maturation. Now George Vaillant follows the men into their

nineties, documenting for the first time what it is like to flourish far beyond conventional retirement. Reporting on all aspects of male life, including relationships, politics and religion, coping strategies, and alcohol use (its abuse being by far the greatest disruptor of health and happiness for the study's subjects), 'Triumphs of Experience' shares a number of surprising findings. For example, the people who do well in old age did not necessarily do so well in midlife, and vice versa. While the study confirms that recovery from a lousy childhood is possible, memories of a happy childhood are a lifelong source of strength. Marriages bring much more contentment after age 70, and physical aging after 80 is determined less by heredity than by habits formed prior to age 50. The credit for growing old with grace and vitality, it seems, goes more to ourselves than to our stellar genetic makeup."

As you can imagine, the study's discoveries are bountiful, but the most significant finding of all is that "Alcoholism is a disorder of great destructive power." In fact, alcoholism is the single strongest cause of divorce between the Grant study men and their wives. Alcoholism was also found to be strongly coupled with neurosis and depression (which most often follows alcohol abuse, rather than preceding it). Together with cigarette smoking, alcoholism proved to be the #1 greatest cause of morbidity and death. And above a certain level, intelligence doesn't prevent the damage.

With regard to income, there was no noticeable difference in maximum income earned by men with

IQs in the 110–115 range vs. men with IQs above 150. With regard to sex lives, one of the most fascinating discoveries is that aging liberals have way more sex. Political ideology had no bearing on overall life satisfaction, but the most conservative men on average shut down their sex lives around age sixty-eight, while the most liberal men had healthy sex lives well into their eighties. Vaillant writes, "I have consulted urologists about this, they have no idea why it might be so."

In *Triumphs of Experience,* Vaillant raises a number of factors more often than others, but the one he refers to most often is the powerful correlation between the warmth of your relationships and your health and happiness in your later years. In 2009, Vaillant's insistence on the importance of this part of the data was challenged, so Vaillant returned to the data to be sure the finding merited such important focus. Not only did Vaillant discover that his focus on warm relationships was warranted, he placed even more importance on this factor than he had previously. Vaillant notes that the fifty-eight men who scored highest on the measurements of "warm relationships" (WR) earned an average of $141,000 a year more during their peak salaries (between ages fifty-five and sixty) than the thirty-one men who scored the lowest in WR. The higher WR scorers were also three times more likely to have professional success worthy of inclusion in Who's Who.

One of the most intriguing discoveries of the Grant Study was how significant men's relationships with their mothers are in determining their well-being in life. For instance, *Business Insider* writes:

"Men who had 'warm' childhood relationships with their mothers took home $87,000 more per year than men whose mothers were uncaring. Men who had poor childhood relationships with their mothers were much more likely to develop dementia when old. Late in their professional lives, the men's boyhood relationships with their mothers—but not their fathers—were associated with effectiveness at work. On the other hand, warm childhood relations with fathers correlated with lower rates of adult anxiety, greater enjoyment on vacations, and increased 'life satisfaction' at age 75— whereas the warmth of childhood relationships with mothers had no significant bearing on life satisfaction at 75."

In Vaillant's own words, the #1 most important finding from the Grant study is this: "The seventy-five years and twenty million dollars expended on the Grant Study points to a straightforward five-word conclusion: Happiness is love. Full stop."[13]

Unfortunately, this study did not follow women. However, is there any doubt that the key to happiness is love? Start pouring your heart and your love into everything you do—your relationships, your work, your entertainment, and your view of life—and you will soon begin to experience the true feeling of happiness.

EXERCISE

➤ What makes you happy?

➤ What things are you naturally good at and enjoy doing?

➤ How can you use your natural strengths to improve your performance in your current position?

➤ What ways can you blend your natural abilities with your natural inclinations to support yourself financially?

➤ What situation could you throw love at?

➤ Identify an opponent or foe. What is one trait you love about them? How can you focus on trying to demonstrate love to that person?

➤ If you didn't have to work for a living, what activities would you like to do all day?

➤ What is your life's purpose?

*"I don't want to work,
I want to bang on the drum all day."*

"BANG THE DRUM ALL DAY," TODD RUNDGREN

CHAPTER ELEVEN

THE PERSISTENCE

*"I will get by,
I will get by,
I will get by,
I will survive."*

"TOUCH OF GREY," THE GRATEFUL DEAD

DID YOU EVER WONDER HOW HISTORY may have turned out differently if Abraham Lincoln packed it in after his myriad of failures and defeats as a small business owner and the loss of Ann Rutledge, the only woman he ever truly loved? What would have happened if Thomas Edison quit trying to invent the light bulb after his first 10,000 tries did not work out? And what might have happened if George Washington—and his troops—surrendered at Valley Forge before their victorious surprise attack on the British? And what will happen to you mentally, emotionally, and physically if you simply quit after suffering defeat or setback? What will happen to your family? What will happen to your legacy?

The reality is that during our journey through life, we all "take a few left hooks to the belly" as my dad was famous for saying. Imagine going to the movies and watching the hero march to victory without any conflict or tension? What fun would that be? There is a reason every movie involving a love story is about boy meeting girl, boy losing girl, and boy winning girl back. Similarly, sports movies are about a team, or an athlete, that suffers defeat before basking in ultimate triumph.

Overcoming setback and temporary defeat is just part of the game we play called life. Steve Miller sums it up aptly in "Jet Airliner":

> *"Ridin' high I got tears in my eyes,*
> *You know you got to go through hell*
> *Before you get to heaven."*

The key to persistence is *faith in your purpose or cause*. When you know what you are aiming for, why you are aiming for it, and when you have faith in your ability to get there (because you are following your light), you will muster the determination, strength, and courage to stick it out through thick and thin. Return to the Grateful Dead lyric that this chapter opens with—*"I will get by, I will survive."* I selected this lyric not only because I love the song "Touch of Grey" but also because if you are reading this right now, you have survived. If you have been through tough times, then you have gotten by and you are a survivor! You may have nowhere to go but up (which is in reality a great and powerful place to start), and you may have had to endure indescribable pain or heartache, but you have survived. The fact that you are reading these words is a testament in and of itself that you are a resilient person who has not given up. That deserves a pat on the back right this very moment!

The people we admire most and the stories we gravitate to are the ones where people have overcome the biggest obstacles to get what they came for in life. They overcame huge odds because they believed. They had light and they let it shine through in everything they did. Their determination to proactively focus their mind on their desired outcome filled their mind, body, and spirit. They had faith that somehow and some way they would realize their chief aim, and it is this quality of persevering that separates these great achievers and makes us worship them. Helen Keller, Beethoven, and Milton all overcame life-limiting physical disabilities and turned those limitations into astounding accomplishments.

If you are feeling down and defeated, then you can take comfort in the wisdom of Napoleon Hill in his inspirational classic *Think and Grow Rich* when he said, "Every adversity, every failure, and every heartache carries with it the Seed of an equivalent or greater Benefit." The importance of this statement cannot be understated. In fact, you may wish to write it down and dwell upon it until you have committed it to memory and allow it to seep into your conscious and subconscious mind. The statement is the truth, and remember that it is the truth that sets you free. If you are searching for faith, you can find it in this single statement alone.

The "Eighth Step toward Riches" that Hill identified in *Think and Grow Rich* is persistence, which he called "the sustained effort necessary to induce faith." He specifically noted that when studying Edison and Ford, he found no other quality save persistence that would otherwise explain their stupendous achievement. Hill also raised the question: "Does the quality of persistence set up in one's mind some form of spiritual, mental, or chemical activity which gives one access to supernatural forces?" After studying the records of hundreds of the most influential individuals across all fields of endeavor from his era, Hill concluded: "As one makes an impartial study of the prophets, philosophers, 'miracle' men, and religious leaders of the past, one is drawn to the inevitable conclusion that PERSISTENCE, concentration of effort, and DEFINITENESS OF PURPOSE, were the major sources of their achievements."

As curious as Hill's statements regarding persistence are, the question arises whether scientific research supports Hill's claims. The answer is yes, and it is well summed up by Dr. Paul T. P. Wong in his article "The Positive Psychology of Persistence and Flexibility":

> What are the most valuable life strategies essential for survival and resilience? What are the most common traits shared by successful athletes and CEOs? More importantly, what are the virtues most important in living the good life? My answer to all the above questions is the same: persistence and flexibility. You need these two virtues to slay your inner dragon and vanquish your deadly foes. Persistence beckons you with eternal hope, while flexibility enables you to get through the obstacles that stand between you and your dreams. If you can understand and apply the positive psychology of persistence and flexibility, then nothing can prevent you from achieving success.

*"And we started from the bottom
now we're here."*

"STARTED FROM THE BOTTOM," DRAKE

When Mimi and I visited Yellowstone Park in the early 1990s, there was still widespread evidence of the 1988 forest fires that burned 63 percent (500,000 acres) of the park. And yet far from catastrophic, fires in Yellowstone are part of the natural cycle that leads to rebirth. As stated in the U.S. National Park Service PDF download titled "The Yellowstone Fires of 1988":

> Fire has been a natural force operating in the Yellowstone ecosystem for thousands of years. The vegetation here is adapted to survive fire and, in some cases, is dependent on it. For example, lodgepole pines produce some cones that open only with intense heat. Some plant communities depend on the light that reaches the forest floor after a fire has killed the thickly spaced trees that shade a mature forest. Cavity-nesting birds, such as bluebirds and woodpeckers, move in after a burn to make their nests and homes in the dead trees.

Additionally, scientists learned that "plant growth was unusually lush in the first years after the fires because ash was rich in minerals and more sunlight reached the forest floors."[14]

Rather than dwell in defeat when you fail at a venture, view the event as a sign of rebirth, rejuvenation, and new growth. When we try something and fail, we learn and we improve. We are then able to narrow our focus on what is working and what is not working. We begin to head in a new direction that is a better path than the one we were on. Taking action and then paying attention to what is and is not working is a great formula for success. Hence, far from feeling dejected after a setback, get excited and make the adjustment necessary to improve your performance and bring you closer to your goal.

If you think you have it bad, let's look at the life cycle of one of the most remarkable journeys of any living creature, the salmon. The Northwest salmon returns to the place of birth in a river or stream far upstream from the ocean in which they spend most of their adult life. Of course, making it downstream to the ocean in the first place is a lesson in overcoming obstacles in and of itself. However, let's look at the adversities that the salmon overcome on their way back to the riverbed of their birth.

First, they are swimming upstream. The average spawning trip distance is about 150 miles. The longest known spawning trip length is from the Bering Sea to Teslin Lake in Canada, a total distance exceeding 2,400 miles and a 2,200-foot elevation gain.[15] On the way upstream, the salmon face fishermen, fish ladders, waterfalls, and more predators, in addition to the challenges they faced on their way downstream earlier in their lives. Humans may have also built more dams or increased river pollution since the downstream journey.

Although salmon do not feed on their way upstream, they can be caught by skillfully presented fishing tackle. In clear water, where the salmon can be seen, it is not uncommon for a fisherman to present his lure dozens of times before sparking the fish's interest enough to take the offering.

Fish ladders are built to provide salmon with a way around hydroelectric dams and other obstructions. They are made of a series of pools arranged in a stair-step fashion. Water falls from step to step, and salmon must jump from one pool to the next to reach the top. Salmon must jump up small waterfalls in rivers the same way they climb fish ladders. Salmon can actually climb waterfalls that are higher than they can jump by swimming and leaping upward through the strong current using their powerful tails.

The predators that salmon face on their journey upstream include bears, wildcats, and eagles. The bones and scraps of salmon left in the forest by these animals fertilize the forest and help it grow.

The salmon also undergo physical changes in their fat composition, skin pigmentation, blood chemistry, enzymes, and hormones.[16] At this stage, they are more susceptible to disease.

The salmon that make it back to their home streams to spawn have beaten amazing odds. On average, out of every 1,000 eggs laid, one survives to return and spawn.

Notice that the salmon has one single mission to pursue. Presumably, the salmon never get discouraged or doubt themselves. Certainly, they never quit! Rather, the salmon keep moving toward their destination regardless of how many obstacles may be in their way. Adopt the same singular focus as the salmon. Yes, that's right—I am suggesting you behave like a fish!

I was once listening to New York Giants Hall of Fame quarterback and now CBS football color commentator, Phil Simms, being interviewed on the radio. At one point during the discussion about his Hall of Fame career, he commented that "most of the time things weren't going well." He explained the many hits he took along the way: criticism, injuries, failed plays, sacks, defeats, and interceptions. Phil Simms was a true professional, though, and his burning desire to seek continuous improvement and reach his end goal of being inducted into the Hall of Fame would not be derailed by any one play or series of plays or games or even a season. The truth is that in life we can only take it one play at a time. If you make a bad play, go on to the next play. If you fall down, then get back up, dust yourself off, and make it your mantra to say, *"Next play."* Remember you are on a mission! The main thing is to keep moving in the direction of your dreams. Martin Luther King Jr. said, "If you can't fly, then run, if you can't run, then walk, if you can't walk, then crawl, but whatever you do, you have to keep moving forward."

In the next chapter, we will inject magic power into your life!

EXERCISE

➤ From now on, every time something does not turn out your way, start searching for the benefit that comes from it.

➤ Remember that new life and new beginnings rise from the ashes of defeat.

➤ Write down the Napoleon Hill quote on page 141 and read it often until you have adopted it into your mind and heart.

➤ Take pride in overcoming adversity like the Pacific salmon.

➤ When things did not work out as you expected them to, adopt the mantra "Next play."

➤ "Don't Give Up . . . Don't Ever Give Up." —Jim Valvano

"I get knocked down, but I get up again
You are never going to keep me down."

"TUBTHUMPING," CHUMBAWAMBA

CHAPTER TWELVE

THE MAGIC POWER

"So turn me on—turn me up—
it's your turn to dream.
A little magic power makes it
better than it seems."

"MAGIC POWER," TRIUMPH

DO YOU BELIEVE IN MAGIC? Once you recognize that overcoming obstacles is just part of the game—and that the harder you fall the higher you will rise—and once you begin to overcome adversity and find the equivalent or greater benefit in the setback, you are able to see miracles happen in your life! Miracles are impossible without faith, and really, who needs a miracle unless it is to overcome or improve upon something? Magic and miracles are the elixir in life that takes you from the ordinary to the extraordinary. Lefty Gomez said, "I'd rather be lucky than good." Gomez happened to have Hall of Fame baseball talent so he was both. I want you to be *good* so when fortune comes your way you can capitalize on it. I think of it as being in the "ready position."

All toil aside, there is magic in this life and to this life, and there is magic in you. In life, there are those whose very existence is filled with the magic of life. These fortunate ones seem to flow through life in harmonious unison with the flow of the universe, and all they touch seemingly turns to gold. They comprise a minute segment of the population. There are others who find their gold at the end of the rainbow but only as the result of severe toil and turmoil. These people also comprise a small portion of the population, and, notwithstanding their seemingly painful journey, they have found their way to abundance. They are to be commended for their resolve and persistence. Far from feeling envious of these fortunate souls, we should emulate them, study them, and determine the manner and the means in which we can live the same magical lifestyle they do. And so, the question becomes, "Why are these people caught up in the magic of life while the rest of us plod through life with something less spectacular?"

The magic in you is a powerful force. It has the force of energy to literally transform your life, your surroundings, and your inner soul in perfect harmony with your deepest desires. Life is energy and you are life. The same energy that lights the sky, moves the rivers, creates the music of an orchestra, and produces the finest art is the same energy that propels you through your existence—either consciously or subconsciously. You can transcend the limits of what is humanly possible if you choose to do so.

Your life is meant to be magical; in fact, it is magical already. You have every bit as much right to tap into the abundance of life as the wealthiest, most talented, and happiest people do. We are all interconnected, and we all deserve to live an opulent lifestyle filled with the glory of God's creation. Your job is to understand this phenomenon, find your dream, and start living it today! Tomorrow will never come, and it's always too late.

This book is part mythical, physical, metaphysical, and pragmatic. Whether you are a pessimist, optimist, pragmatic, dreamer, or naysayer, here is an answer to your dreams and prayers, which are part of the Universe. Your job is to keep the faith; find, follow, and feel your light; maintain your desire; love; stay upbeat; keep your chin up; and remain persistent and consistent in your activity. Then stay alert for the things that make sense and feel good. The rest will come with the natural and orderly laws of the Universe as surely as the night follows the day.

Begin with *your* grandest end in mind and travel through the minds and ages of the greatest men and women who have tapped into this Universal and magical flow of life and realized their greatest ambitions come to fruition. Verily, the same magic in them is the same magic that resides in you. As you go forth from here, never forget the most basic tenet: all creation and achievement of man began with human thought. The human mind is in and of itself the stuff of which magic is made.

"This magic moment . . . will last forever, forever until the end of time."

"THIS MAGIC MOMENT," THE DRIFTERS

The one with the most magic moments wins. Think about it. Your life is meant to be an extraordinary journey filled with magical moments that electrify your soul. Whatever may be said of martyrdom, your purpose is to create for yourself an opulent and abundant life that you can then share with others. A life filled with peace, joy, happiness, excitement, and harmony is yours for the taking. The more you have, the more you can give. The abundant parent who can aptly provide for his or her family maintains a sense of joy and contentment, while the parent who is unable to do so may feel inferior, frustrated, disappointed, and dejected.

God, or if you prefer the Infinite, is not some disinterested presence hanging out in some faraway place in the sky. Instead, God resides in you. The Infinite through your subconscious mind (as directed by your conscious mind) can unleash the magic and miracles you desire. Life so lived then becomes a magical mystical ride where your deepest desires are fulfilled. In this way, you can find the rhythm of your soul and have the peace of mind and confidence that best serves you and your fellow man. If you doubt this, listen to the Lord who says, "What things soever you desire, when ye pray, believe that ye receive them, and ye shall have them." (Mark 11:24, KJV).

Return to chapter 7 and revisit or make a list of all the things you wish to have, be, or do while on this Earth. Do not bother yourself with whether your wants and dreams are realistic or how you could possibly accomplish them. Do not fret that you may be broke, depressed, and seemingly moving further away rather than closer to your dreams. You create your own reality by way of your feelings, thoughts, actions, and the results you are experiencing. By simply making your wish list, you can instantly stop the backward trend and send a vibration into the Universe. Now that the dreams inside your mind and heart are written down, they are a part of the outside world. Congratulations, you just established positive momentum. Look for the magic and miracles as your dreams begin to manifest themselves.

The root thought of human accomplishment is man's desire to achieve and grow, which emanated through a thought impulse. One thought or idea expressed by a firm decision becomes a cause set in motion. If it's a good idea, it will lead to good results; conversely, if it's a bad idea (e.g., the Darwin Awards), it can lead to catastrophic results. Plant high-quality ideas in your mind and let them produce high-quality results. If you doubt this, study the records of the greatest names in history who began with no other tool at their disposal than a definite decision to move in the direction of their dream.

Abraham Lincoln could not cut it as a small businessman, but once he became president (by communicating excellent ideas), his individual desire saved the nation and freed the slaves. O. Henry was a jailed embezzler and world-renowned author whose writings have withstood the test of time. What would have happened to the history of rock-and-roll music if John Lennon "thought" he had no shot of becoming perhaps the most prolific songwriter and artist in the twentieth century? If you have not yet begun to find, feel, and follow your light, this is the time to start!

"God have mercy on the man
Who doubts what he's sure of."
"BRILLIANT DISGUISE," BRUCE SPRINGSTEEN

Your time to shine is now. Don't be the man that Bruce Springsteen references in the above lyric. Deep down inside you know what you really want, you know who you really want to be, and you know the places you really want to go. There is no time left to hesitate or to let doubt drag you down. Don't be the person who is to be pitied because he doubted what he was sure of. Be a victor, not a victim! This ability to go for what you want no matter how fearful or reluctant you may be is the real test of courage and the key that unlocks the magic power of the Universe!

Do not let the fear of failure, the fear of success, or the feeling of guilt weigh you down. The material substance of the world is for all to share and have. By getting you can give, by learning you can teach, and by doing you can inspire.

Andrew Carnegie ranks as one of the most accomplished businessmen and philanthropists the world has ever seen. His name graces the world's most famous music hall in New York City (Carnegie Hall), a top-tier university in Pittsburgh (Carnegie Mellon University), and countless libraries. His philosophy was simple: Spend the first third of your life learning, the next third earning as much as you can, and the last third giving away all that you have acquired to the less fortunate. He did exactly that; he shared both his material wealth and his knowledge toward the end of his life. He was not a perfect man, and there were blemishes on his record. However, do you not think that the Universe is proud of Carnegie?

If you have never really believed in magic or in miracles, it's time to open up your mind and explore the possibilities–you may just be dazzled.

EXERCISE

➤ Choose one thing you want to have and then look for signs that the Universe is unexpectedly delivering it to you.

➤ Act as if you already have what you want and that you are living the life you have imagined. Then expect and look for the magic and miracles to appear in your life.

➤ Revisit a time in your past when something magically appeared in your life. What can you do to re-create the same feelings and thoughts you had then? How can you apply that state of being to a present situation where magic or miracles are needed?

➤ Identify a limiting belief that has been holding you back. Then, ask the Universe for the magic or miracle that will lead to a breakthrough and obliterate the limiting belief.

➤ Expect a miracle to happen in your life today (i.e., have faith) and then keep an eye out (i.e., focus) for it to manifest.

➤ Focus on and enjoy the magic moments in your life!

"I never did believe in miracles
But I've a feeling it's time to try
I never did believe in the ways of magic
But I'm beginning to wonder why."
"YOU MAKE LOVING FUN," FLEETWOOD MAC

CHAPTER THIRTEEN

THE CELEBRATION

"Celebrate good times, come on!
(It's a celebration)
Celebrate good times, come on!
(Let's celebrate)."

"CELEBRATION," KOOL & THE GANG

THE WORK, THE DREAMS, AND THE PROCESSES have been set in place. You have identified your dream life and you are visualizing living that life and acting as if it has already arrived. Your actions are inspired and your positive energy is vibrating through the Universe. The law of attraction is showing signs of creating magic in your life. Now, it's time to reward yourself by taking a step back and celebrating your progress as your dream life unfolds.

How do you wish to celebrate? Continuing with the lyrics from Kool & the Gang's song "Celebration:" "It's up to you, what's your pleasure?" It can be a big cele-bration like a vacation to an exotic destination, or it can be a small gesture of self-love, like taking a break and watching a movie. In point of fact, taking time to smell the roses should be a primary focus in your life and should be practiced regularly, on a daily basis if possible. Perhaps you can review your "thing" goals and purchase one of the items on your list. Alternatively, consider scheduling a day for yourself and spend it in quiet solitude. Regardless of how you define "celebration," you simply must take the time and spend the energy on rewarding yourself. Remember that on the seventh day the Lord rested.

Celebration is important for a few reasons. First, it serves as positive reinforcement. As your brain begins to link up your achievements with pleasure, you will be spurred on to more progress. Second, by doing something you enjoy, you are honoring yourself and demonstrating self-love and self-worth, which is deeply satisfying. Make yourself a priority! Pat yourself on the back because you are proving to yourself that you find yourself a worthy person. Third, life is really about finding happiness and fun! So, go for it! Napoleon Hill said, "Happiness is found in doing, not merely possessing."

There is yet another very important reason why you need to take time to celebrate—even if you earn your living through *inspired action* and not work. The time away not only allows you to recharge your batteries but also to refocus your activity. The default part of the brain is the daydream part, and scientific studies have revealed that people who "daydream" are more productive than their "grind it out" counterparts. Time away allows you to see the forest for the trees and allows you to make new distinctions that can greatly accelerate your progress. When you are doing something that relaxes you, you are more open to receiving the vibrational energy that can lead to transformation and breakthrough.

In *Think and Grow Rich*, Napoleon Hill emphasizes that simply working hard is not the recipe for accumulating riches. In fact, the accumulation of riches is often produced more by thought consciousness than by burning the midnight oil.

What, then, is the best way to celebrate life? Dr. Robert A. Emmons, professor of psychology at the University of California, Davis, and the founding editor in chief of the *Journal of Positive Psychology* conducted experiments on the impacts of living with gratitude. One of the conclusions from his research was that "those who celebrate life by practicing an attitude of gratitude tend to be more creative, bounce back more quickly from adversity, have a stronger immune system and have stronger social relationships than those who don't practice gratitude."[17]

Don't wait until tomorrow to begin the celebration of life. Regardless of your economic situation, begin at once to keep a gratitude journal and count your blessings. You don't need fortune or fame to find happiness. All you need is love and gratitude, and you will begin to celebrate the riches of life from a new perspective—even when things are not going your way. Remember, focus on the positive and hold on to your faith even in times of trouble. Let's revisit the lyric from Twisted Sister that ended the Preface to this book: "This is our life, this is our song."

EXERCISE

➤ Recognize whatever progress you have made and celebrate that achievement.

➤ Define what "celebration" means to you.

➤ Do you like indoor or outdoor activities?

➤ What ways can you celebrate that cost little or no money?

➤ Review your "goals" list and pick out an activity and do it! Or buy something on your "thing" list.

➤ Start a daily gratitude journal and spend a few minutes each day counting your blessings, even when life is presenting you with challenges.

➤ Be grateful for life's difficulties and challenges. It is these life events that strengthen faith, promote self-growth, and ultimately lead to feelings of self-worth and self-fulfillment.

➤ Party like the rock star that you are!

"I'm free to do what I want and have a good time."

"FREEDOM," PITBULL

CHAPTER FOURTEEN

THE ANSWER

*"The answer, my friend, is blowin' in the wind,
The answer is blowin' in the wind."*

"BLOWIN' IN THE WIND," BOB DYLAN

EVERY ANSWER TO EVERY QUESTION lies within you or at your fingertips. The people who make the "great discoveries" in life tend to be the people who confront a situation they *want* to overcome. They have *faith* that there is a solution, visualize a desired outcome, and *focus* their attention on finding an answer. Their creative instincts kick in as their brain searches for a way to manifest their inner vision. Successful people don't quit until they get the result they want. The real answer in life is to know what you want, and then go get it. If you are looking for an answer to anything that is of interest to you, then take a look ahead, take a look around, and take a look within—using your light at all times.

If I were the speaker at my daughter Lindsay's upcoming graduation at the University of Pennsylvania, or any other college or high school, I would begin by applauding the graduates for their extraordinary accomplishment. I would remind them of how blessed they are for having the unique opportunity to gain an education and become a graduate. I would tell the graduates to be grateful and to be proud of their accomplishments. I would also instruct the graduates to give a standing ovation and applaud all those around them—their family, their friends, their professors, and their classmates, for there is truly no such thing as a "self-made person."

I would also tell the graduates to take time to celebrate their momentous occasion. Life, as imperfect or as difficult as it may be at times, is meant to be enjoyed. Life should be savored and life should be celebrated. I would also suggest to the graduates that they reflect back upon their four years and think about the good times, the difficult times, and the times they were searching for an answer to a relationship, an exam question, or any other life situation they encountered. I would ask that they reassess the situation and think about what was gained and learned from the situation.

I would then tell them, however, that if their greatest accomplishment is graduating from high school or college, then they have not squeezed all the juice out of life. They have not reached for their full potential and they have not followed their light all the way through. A milestone is just the launching point to future growth. I would suggest that the graduates begin the next chapter of their life by *focusing* on what it is they wish to become and not just what they want. I would drop in a quote from Oprah Winfrey: "Passion is energy. Feel the power that comes from focusing on what excites you."

We tend to experience in life that which we focus upon the most. By narrowing your focus to a singular cause and by employing your natural talents to pursue that cause, you not only achieve but also become. Gandhi pursued peace and in the process became a peacemaker. Michael Jordan strived to become the best basketball player in the world and in the process also became a champion. Bruce Springsteen focused on mastering rock and roll and became a rock-and-roll legend. What is it that you want to do and what is it that you wish to become?

WHAT IS THE ANSWER TO
A LIFE WELL LIVED?

"Everybody is a genius. But if you judge a fish by its ability to climb a tree, it will live its whole life believing that it is stupid."

ALBERT EINSTEIN

Whether you are a graduate, a grandparent, or a high school student, I invite you to consider your life's true purpose and ask you to invest your time in quiet solitude and dwell upon the following questions and statements:

1. What are your natural talents?

2. How can you continue to develop your unique talents to serve others?

3. What activities give you joy or excitement?

4. Identify your values.

5. Are you transactional oriented or relationship oriented?

6. What other values do you possess that serve to conflict with the values you identified?

7. Find a greater purpose. (Contribute your talents to the world.)

8. Develop your physical, spiritual, emotional, and intellectual needs.

9. Become aware of your surroundings (situational awareness).

10. Let life unfold—let it be!

11. What do you want your legacy to be?

"Still at the end of every hard day
people find some reason to believe."
"REASON TO BELIEVE," BRUCE SPRINGSTEEN

Recall from chapter 11 that *persistence* is what Napoleon Hill called "the sustained effort necessary to induce faith." To get from where you are to where you want to be, you must be willing to stay the course. Most great accomplishments are borne from consistent and persistent activity rather than one great action. To stay the course, we must believe that our actions are carrying us closer to our target. We must have a strong enough belief system to keep us moving when times get tough. Thomas Edison remained vigilant in order to invent the light bulb because he maintained faith after each failed attempt. His invention was years and thousands of failed attempts in the making. Follow your light, maintain your vision, listen to your positive inner voice of faith, keep a flow of good vibrations, and keep moving toward what you want. All you need is a strong enough reason to believe and to stay the course in life (regardless of how many times you have suffered a temporary setback). This is the stuff of which life is made.

"The quality of a person's life is in direct proportion to their commitment to excellence, regardless of their chosen field of endeavor."
VINCE LOMBARDI

You see, for the greatest achievers in this world, it's not about where they are, what they have, or what they have already accomplished. It's all about mastery and commitment to excellence in a chosen field. Choosing that field is a momentous decision, for if blended with your natural talents, it will provide the passion necessary to fuel any great undertaking. For great achievers, it's more about how much better they can become in their chosen path, through self-improvement and self-awareness, than it is about any one achievement or accolade. What you focus on most in life is what you will experience the most in life. If you could choose to become one thing in life, what would it be? What work or activities fill your soul 100 percent?

> *"If you have a high expectation of yourself without a high level of commitment, then expect a high level of frustration."*
> JOHN McCLAIN, AMERICAN HERITAGE
> BOCA/DELRAY HIGH SCHOOL'S GIRLS
> LACROSSE HEAD COACH

Is there any wonder that John McClain, my daughter Megan's lacrosse coach, is among the best high school lacrosse coaches in the country? John doesn't just set high expectations for himself and his players, he has and makes sure his players have the high level of commitment to match those high standards. If you have high expectations but do not have the corresponding level of commitment that it takes to achieve your goals, then you are setting yourself up for self-defeat. It is when you fully immerse yourself in your cause, such that you are living the dream, that you encounter the miracles and magic along the way. Finding the balance between setting and achieving goals and managing your expectations is the difference between self-satisfaction versus self-defeat.

Life really is more about the journey and then celebrating the destination long enough to feel the fulfillment and self-satisfaction that leads to feeling significant. Harken back to Marianne Williamson's words in which she states that you do not serve the world by playing small. You best serve the word and yourself by letting your light shine. You best serve the world and those around you by relying upon your faith to overcome your fears. You best serve the world by attacking life rather than, as Bruce Springsteen says, "Spend half your life just covering up." Life is meant to be lived—so don't fear it . . . go live it!

Then, once a milestone is reached, it's about choosing the next milestone and embarking upon a new journey that was discovered by following your light. For many of us, it's not about accomplishment. It's more about becoming absorbed in something in life that provides you with energy and joy. It's about following your light toward happiness and using your light to lead you through the dark moments in life that we all face from time to time. It's about having a cause—like being a single parent to a couple of kids—that is bigger than yourself and makes the sacrifices you make worth it at the end of the day. It gives you a reason to go on.

DOING AND BEING

Our society is filled with "doing." Action is what brings you to your target. However, by immersing yourself in an activity, you not only reach a destination, you become something as a result. The real challenge in life is to dwell more upon "being" and not just about "doing." It's about living the dream long before it ever comes true and enjoying the ride. The answers are indeed blowing in the wind. The spirit abounds. When life presents its greatest challenges, don't overdo it; let it be. Keep the faith and let it be. There would be less neurosis in our society and less anxiety if we would all simply allow each individual to feel and follow their light. We would all be better off individually and as a society if we make it our mantra to empower others to feel better about themselves and empower ourselves to feel better about ourselves. That is the secret—the only real magic to living a happy, meaningful, and impactful life. Whether you help millions like Gandhi or help just your elderly parent, the hunger to make you and others feel good is magic. Find and follow your light, and go forth with faith and focus—with a smile on your face, love in your heart, and your vision in mind. Stay the course. Listen to your inner voice.

If you are wondering where to begin or where to look, start from where you are at right now. Most "great ideas"—the multimillion-dollar type—are all around you. You don't have to search far and wide for the next great thing. It is showing up in your daily existence every day; whatever it is, you are attracting it into your life. If it is a recurring problem, then figure out how to solve the problem, and you can then market your solution to a large segment of the population that is encountering the same issue.

For progress to take place, you must have faith. You must recognize that regardless of your present situation—whether it be health, family, or finances—you hold the power and, indeed, the responsibility to make decisions today that will benefit you in the future. Your faith will not only strengthen your focus; it will strengthen you as well. Stay the course in life. Focus your energy on your natural God-given strengths and follow your inclinations. Norman Vincent Peale said, "Drop the idea that you are Atlas carrying the world on your shoulders.

The world would go on even without you. Don't take yourself so seriously." Do what comes naturally to you and leave what doesn't to others. Throw love into every action, thought, and gesture you make.

Martin Luther King Jr. said: "Take the first step in faith. You don't have to see the whole staircase, just take the first step." Don't let fear or uncertainty or even laziness hold you back or stifle your progress. Let your faith be stronger than your fear.

As you embark upon your life's journey, you must figure out if you are transactional in nature or relationship centered. In my experience, the transactional types often fare better in the short run but oftentimes end up unhappy. Relationship-driven people, conversely, tend to thrive over the long run. They have a long-term view of things and are not looking to "score" with every new transaction. They often lose the battle with an eye toward winning the war. They understand innately that there are ties that bind each of us together.

Decide what it is you want from life, have a plan to get it, and then adopt a manner in which you will pursue your passion. Are you out to help others so that all parties can benefit from a transaction, or are you driven solely by the possession of things or other people? If the latter, I recommend that you proceed with caution. Simply study the record of the world's historical leaders, most of whom ended up in tragic defeat–Napoleon, Caesar, and Alexander the Great, to name a few. There truly is something to the old proverb "Live by the sword, die by the sword."

What Do You Want Your Legacy to Be?

*"I heard you die twice, once when
they bury you in the grave
And the second time is the last time
that somebody mentions your name."*

"GLORIOUS," MACKLEMORE

How do you wish to be remembered? What do you want your legacy to be? When deciding upon what you want in life, take into consideration how it is you wish to be remembered by your family, friends, and colleagues and in general. Do you wish to be a net taker or a net giver? Will you leave the world a better place? How? What will be your lasting contribution to society? Paint a picture in your mind of how you wish to be remembered, and let this vision guide your actions and interactions with others.

In chapter 1, we talked about the universal nature of your light. You were instructed to find and follow your light and let it shine through in everything you do. You were asked to contemplate that there is a universal energy field that permeates the Universe and that we are all connected to and part of this radiant energy field. From that radiant field comes your light. The light you have is the same light that brightens the sky, the stars, and the galaxies. We have come full circle, then, because while you are allowing your light to shine, the same universal light is shining down on you. Wherever you go in life, whatever you do, and whatever happens to you, know that the light that shines within you is the same light that shines upon you. It will be with you always. Connect your light within to the light without and you will find harmony and divinity. The answer was there all along. With your light, you will never be alone. Go forth and let it shine and let it be.

"And in my hour of darkness . . .
there is still a light that shines on me
Shine until tomorrow, let it be . . .
Let it be, let it, let it be, let it be,
There will be an answer, let it be."

"LET IT BE," THE BEATLES

EXERCISE

➤ What is it that you want to do and what is it that you wish to become?

➤ What are your natural talents?

➤ What are the things in life that you do and enjoy so much that time just slips on by?

➤ What are the activities that feed your soul 100 percent?

➤ Decide upon the one thing you want the most and begin at once to visualize its manifestation.

➤ What do you want your legacy to be?

➤ Focus on answers to the issues you are currently confronting.

> Focus on your results in pursuit of your dreams.

> Write down in detail the life you want to live.

> Focus on becoming the person you want to be.

> Don't deprive yourself of the pleasures of life, even if life is hard, confusing, or unfair.

> Feel the power and energy that arises when you pursue your passion.

> Be grateful for what you have, even if what you think you have is not all that great.

> Don't fear life; have faith, and attack life!

> Pursue your passion and let it be!

> Have faith and focus always!

> Let your light shine!

ACKNOWLEDGMENTS

WHERE DO I BEGIN TO EXPRESS MY GRATITUDE and say thank you to all the people in my life who got me to the point of believing that I could write a book, and then to all those who helped me with the actual writing and publishing of the book?

Let me first begin with my wife. Mimi, we have been through so much together. Thank you for believing in me and for being the best mother that a man could ever ask for his kids to have. I love you.

To my children, Austin, Lindsay, and Megan. Each of you has brought so much joy to my life, and I have learned so much from each of you. Austin, you have always done it your way—it is with pride that you appear on the cover of this book and that I got to quote one of your lyrics; Lindsay, your were my confidant throughout and your editorial and writing skills proved invaluable, as did your enthusiastic support; Megan, you gave me some great ideas at the end and helped push me over the goal line. Each of you are letting your individual lights shine and you are each glowing examples of faith with focus.

To my late parents, Tom and Phyllis, and to all my brothers and sisters: I was so lucky to be "the little bro" of the family even if it meant I was the "buck private." You have all enriched my life in countless ways. Thank you.

To all my friends from childhood, high school, college, law school, and beyond, all too numerous to mention. There is no doubt that some of you are saying to yourself, "You, Brian? I had no idea!" Well, now you know that deep down an author was lurking within me. A special nod to my departed high school friend, Tom Raslovsky, whose spirit shall live on forever. There are many songs quoted in this book that remind me of all of you and the good old days.

To my friend, Attorney Margaret Young. Micki, you were the first person to read the opening chapters. Your feedback inspired me to keep writing! There were several others who also read parts of my book, for which I wish to thank you all collectively. Special thanks to Julia Porter, who provided valuable feedback, and to Becky Bumgardner of the V Foundation for Cancer Research. Thank you to all my fellow members at WCR Palm Beaches Noon Toastmasters. All of you are amazing and your contributions helped me more than you'll ever know.

To my paralegal, Maria Lord, who kept me on track and supported me throughout this process. And, of course, a special thanks to The Book Couple, Carol and Gary Rosenberg, whose skill, patience, and encouragement turned my words into a book!

SUGGESTED RESOURCES

Books and Audio Books

Allen, James. *As a Man Thinketh*

Assaraf, John and Smith, Murray. *The Answer*

Byrne, Rhonda. *The Secret*

Byrne, Rhonda. *The Hero*

Canfield, Jack and Switzer, Janet. *The Success Principles*

Cohen, Alan. *A Course in Miracles Made Easy* (Audio Book)

Steven Covey. *The Seven Habits of Highly Successful People*

Dooley, Mike. *Playing the Matrix* (Unabridged Audio Book)

Dooley, Mike. *Manifesting Change, It Couldn't Be Easier* (Unabridged Audio Book)

Dyer Wayne. *The Secrets of the Power of Intention* (Hay House: Audible 2006–2007)

Dyer, Wayne. *Excuses Begone* (Audio book)

Dyer, Wayne. *Wishes Fulfilled*

Dyer, Wayne. *Change Your Thoughts Change Your Mind: Living the Wisdom of the Tao*

Goddard, Neville. *The Power of Awareness*

Haanel, Charles. *The Master Key System*

Hill, Napoleon. *Think and Grow Rich*. New York: Fawcett Books (1987)

Maxwell, John. *Make Today Count*

Murphy, Joseph. *Maximize Your Potential Through the Power of Your Subconscious Mind for an Enriched Life: Book 6.* Hay House Classics (2008)

Murphy, Joseph. *Maximize Your Potential to Create Wealth and Success.* Dr. Joseph Murphy (Gildan Media LLC: Audible, 2012)

Earl Nightingale. *The Strangest Secret*

Osteen, Joel. *The Power of I Am: Two Words That Will Change Your Life Today*

Peale, Norman Vincent. *The Power of Positive Thinking*

Proctor, Bob. *You Were Born Rich* (Audio Book)

Robbins, Tony. *Unleash the Power Within*

Thoreau, David. *Walden*

Tolle, Eckhart. *The Power of Now: A Guide to Spiritual Enlightenment*

Vitale, Joe. *The Awaking Course* (Audio Book)

Ziglar, Zig. *Developing the Qualities of Success, How to Stay Motivated* (Audio Book)

Online Resources

(Business Insider. "Why Is the 'God Particle' Such a Big Deal?" July 5, 2012. Accessed September 4, 2018. www.businessinsider.com/why-is-the-god-particle-such-a-big-deal-2012-7.)

The Two Kinds of Belief: Why Infants Reason Better than Adults. Post published by Alex Lickerman M.D., on April 24, 2011 in *Happiness in this World.*

Fredrickson, Barbara L. "The Role of Positive Emotions in Positive Psychology: The Broaden-and-Build Theory of Positive Emotions." American Psychologist 56, no. 3 (March 2001):218–226. www.ncbi.nlm.nih.gov/pubmed/11315248.

Williamson, Marianne. *A Return to Love: Reflections on the Principles of "A Course in Miracles."* San Francisco, CA: HarperOne, 1996.

Mike Dooley. "Notes from the Universe" (daily emails)

Robbins, Stever. "How to Set Goals for the Life You Actually Want." Fast

Company. April 29, 2014. Accessed September 4, 2018. www.fastcompany. com/3029765/work-smart/how-to-set-goals-for-the-life-you-actually-want.

Jonathan Milligan, founder of Blogging Your Passion.

Investopedia. "Opportunity Cost." Accessed September 6, 2018. www. investopedia.com/terms/o/opportunitycost.asp#ixzz4z56rbt00.

Canfield, Jack. "Creating 'Miracles' with the Rule of Five." Jack Canfield: Maximizing Your Potential. Accessed September 6, 2018. jackcanfield.com/blog/creating-miracles-with-the-rule-of-five/.

Ferri, Rick. "Set It and Forget It Works." Forbes. June 11, 2015. Accessed September 6, 2018. www.forbes.com/sites/rickferri/2015/06/11/set-it-and-forget-it-works/#2b69b5746285

Lambert, Brent. "75 Years in The Making: Harvard Just Released its Epic Study on What Men Need to Live a Happy Life." FeelGuide. April 29, 2013. Accessed September 6, 2018.www.feelguide.com/2013/04/29/75-years-harvard-happiness-epic-study-men-happy-life/.

National Park Service. "The Yellowstone Fires of 1988." Accessed September 6, 2018/ www.nps.gov/yell/learn/nature/upload/firesupplement.pdf.

http://www.washingtontourist.com/salmon/journey/six.html

Booth, Janice Holly. "Why It's Important to Celebrate. A Lot." AARP. Accessed September 6, 2018. www.aarp.org/health/healthy-living/info-2017/celebrate-life-attitude-of-gratitude.html.

ENDNOTES

1 "Everybody's beautiful in their own way."—"Everything Is Beautiful," Ray Stevens.

2 In 1964, scientist Dr. Peter Higgs began describing the theory of a common particle or energy source existent throughout and in all things that make up the Universe. In July 2012, scientists at the European Organization for Nuclear Research, or CERN, announced the finding of a new subatomic particle with 99.99997 percent certainty which is a near-perfect fit for what physicists have expected of the Higgs boson. Simplistically, the Higgs boson has been described as follows: "It's the physical proof of an invisible, universe-wide field that gave mass to all matter right after the Big Bang, forcing particles to coalesce into stars, planets, and everything else. If the Higgs field, and Higgs boson, didn't exist, the dominant Standard Model of particle physics would be wrong." ("Why Is the 'God Particle' Such a Big Deal?" *Business Insider,* July 5, 2012. Accessed September 4, 2018. www.businessinsider.com/why-is-the-god-particle-such-a-big-deal-2012-7.)

3 Gavin D. Flood, *An Introduction to Hinduism*. Cambridge University Press, 1996.

4 Alex Lickerman. "Two Kinds of Belief Why Infants Reason Better than Adults," *Psychology Today,* April 24, 2011. Accessed September 15, 2018. https://www.psychologytoday.com/us/blog/happiness-in-world/201104/the-two-kinds-belief.

5 Fredrickson, Barbara L. "The Role of Positive Emotions in Positive Psychology: The Broaden-and-Build Theory of Positive Emotions." *American Psychologist* 56, no. 3 (March 2001):218–226. www.ncbi.nlm.nih.gov/pubmed/11315248.

6 This is the exact quote from Thoreau's book *Walden.* Today, the quote is most widely stated like this: "Go confidently in the direction of your dreams. Live the life that you have imagined."

7 Marianne Williamson. *A Return to Love: Reflections on the Principles of "A Course in Miracles."* San Francisco, CA: HarperOne, 1996.

8 Stever Robbins. "How to Set Goals for the Life You Actually Want." *Fast Company.* April 29, 2014. Accessed September 4, 2018. www.fastcompany.com/3029765/work-smart/how-to-set-goals-for-the-life-you-actually-want.

9 From Mike Dooley's *Notes from the Universe.*

10 Investopedia. "Opportunity Cost." Accessed September 6, 2018. www.investopedia.com/terms/o/opportunitycost.asp#ixzz4z56rbt00.

11 Jack Canfield. "Creating 'Miracles' with the Rule of Five." *Jack Canfield: Maximizing Your Potential.* Accessed September 6, 2018. jackcanfield.com/blog/creating-miracles-with-the-rule-of-five/.

12 Rick Ferri. "Set It and Forget It Works." *Forbes,* June 11, 2015. Accessed September 6, 2018. www.forbes.com/sites/rickferri/2015/06/11/set-it-and-forget-it-works/#2b69b5746285

13 Brent Lambert. "75 Years in the Making: Harvard Just Released its Epic Study on What Men Need to Live a Happy Life." *FeelGuide.* April 29, 2013. Accessed September 6, 2018. www.feelguide.com/2013/   04/29/75-years-harvard-happiness-epic-study-men-happy-life/.

14 National Park Service. "The Yellowstone Fires of 1988." Accessed September 6, 2018. www.nps.gov/yell/learn/nature/upload/fire supplement.pdf.

15 Edward C. Migdalski, George S. Fichter, Norman Weaver. *The Fresh & Salt Water Fishes of the World.* New York, NY: Greenwich House, 1989, 116–117.

16 Robert Steelquist. *Field Guide to the Pacific Salmon.* Seattle, WA: Sasquatch, 1994, 43.

17 Janice Holly Booth. "Why It's Important to Celebrate. A Lot." AARP. Accessed September 6, 2018. www.aarp.org/health/healthy-living/info -2017/celebrate-life-attitude-of-gratitude.html.

ABOUT THE AUTHOR

Brian Mangines, J.D., LL.M, is an estate planning and probate attorney residing in Boca Raton, Florida. Growing up the youngest of eight children in Trumbull, Connecticut, Brian learned from an early age the importance of having strong interpersonal skills, faith, and focus to successfully navigate the trials and tribulations of life. Brian received his undergraduate degree from Cornell University, his law degree from the University of Connecticut, School of Law, and his master of law degree from the University of Miami, School of Law.

Over the years, both as an entrepreneur and an attorney, Brian has helped his clients successfully navigate through some of life's greatest challenges such as the death of a loved one, job loss, bankruptcy, foreclosure, divorce, and litigation. As an estate planning attorney, Brian is passionate about helping his clients protect what matters most to them: their families, their finances, and their legacy. What he learned from his myriad of experiences is that having impenetrable faith (however that word may be individually defined) and a keen focus upon what one wants are the keys to living a happy, fulfilling, and purposeful life.

Brian has been married to his law school sweetheart, Mimi, since 1990. Together they have three children, Austin, Lindsay, and Megan. Brian enjoys long-distance running, golf, fishing, and reading.

45222673R00108

Made in the USA
Middletown, DE
15 May 2019